Local Boards of Health

in North Carolina

KIRSTEN E. LELOUDIS

UNC SCHOOL OF GOVERNMENT

The School of Government at the University of North Carolina at Chapel Hill works to improve the lives of North Carolinians by engaging in practical scholarship that helps public officials and citizens understand and improve state and local government. Established in 1931 as the Institute of Government, the School provides educational, advisory, and research services for state and local governments. The School of Government is also home to a nationally ranked Master of Public Administration program, the North Carolina Judicial College, and specialized centers focused on community and economic development, information technology, and environmental finance.

As the largest university-based local government training, advisory, and research organization in the United States, the School of Government offers up to 200 courses, webinars, and specialized conferences for more than 12,000 public officials each year. In addition, faculty members annually publish approximately 50 books, manuals, reports, articles, bulletins, and other print and online content related to state and local government. The School also produces the *Daily Bulletin Online* each day the General Assembly is in session, reporting on activities for members of the legislature and others who need to follow the course of legislation.

Operating support for the School of Government's programs and activities comes from many sources, including state appropriations, local government membership dues, private contributions, publication sales, course fees, and service contracts.

Visit sog.unc.edu or call 919.966.5381 for more information on the School's courses, publications, programs, and services.

Some chapters in this book appeared in slightly different form in *Local Social Services Boards in North Carolina*, by Kristi A. Nickodem (UNC School of Government, 2023), and *Consolidated Human Services Boards in North Carolina*, by Kristi A. Nickodem and Kirsten E. Leloudis (UNC School of Government, 2025).

Printed in the United States of America
29 28 27 26 25 1 2 3 4 5
ISBN 978-1-64238-111-5

To all the public health workers
who labor day in and day out, often behind
the scenes, to keep us all safer and healthier—
thank you.

Contents

Preface

Local Boards of Health in North Carolina is a new resource from the UNC School of Government, published with the goal of providing the hundreds of volunteers who serve on boards of health across the state with the information that they need to conduct their work lawfully, effectively, and with confidence. This book may also be of help and interest to local health directors, county attorneys, county commissioners, county managers, and others working in governmental public health.

This book is an installment in a three-part series that also includes *Local Social Services Boards in North Carolina,* by Kristi A. Nickodem, and a forthcoming book written for consolidated human services boards. More School of Government resources regarding social services, public health, and consolidated human services can be found at the North Carolina Human Services hub at humanservices.sog.unc.edu.

Local Boards of Health builds on decades of research, writing, and teaching by Jill Moore. Portions of this book are adapted from her 2018 piece titled "Local Boards of Health in North Carolina: Overview of Membership Requirements and Legal Authorities."[1] In addition to the work that laid the foundations for this book, I am indebted to Jill for the many hours she spent reviewing draft book chapters and talking through my questions. I am appreciative of her mentorship and the generosity with which she has shared her time and expertise since I joined the faculty here at the School.

I am also grateful to Aimee Wall and Kristi Nickodem for their work on human services agencies in North Carolina. For this book, Kristi not only contributed multiple chapters but also reviewed early drafts of many of the book's other sections. It was her idea to produce a three-part book series for local boards of social services, boards of health, and consolidated human services boards. None of this would be possible without her.

I would also like to thank my fellow School of Government faculty members Crista Cuccaro, Kristina Wilson, and Rebecca Fisher-Gabbard, as well as external legal and public health experts including Virginia Niehaus, Stacie Saunders, John Schaeffer, Margaret Benson Nemitz, and Merle Green, for the helpful review and feedback that they provided for various sections of this book.

1. Jill D. Moore, *Local Boards of Health in North Carolina: Overview of Membership Requirements and Legal Authorities* (UNC School of Government, Mar. 2018), https://perma.cc/XA6C-7T89.

Many thanks are also due to the myriad state and local public health workers who have brought me their thoughtful, challenging legal questions and who have been so patient, generous, and helpful when I came to them with questions of my own. Their inquiries and counsel about how public health gets done on the ground have helped inform the substance of this book.

I must also thank my village, including my family (in particular, JP, Theo, Jim, Dianne, and Rebecca) and my friends. Your love, support, and encouragement are everything.

Finally, I am grateful to the people of North Carolina, whose support makes my and the School's work possible. It is an honor, privilege, and absolute pleasure to get to do this work. Thank you.

Kirsten E. Leloudis
Assistant Professor of Public Law and Government
The University of North Carolina at Chapel Hill
June 2025

Commonly Used Abbreviations

BOCC	board of county commissioners
BOH	local board of health
CHS	consolidated human services
CHSA	consolidated human services agency
CPH	North Carolina Commission for Public Health
DCFW	North Carolina Division of Child and Family Well-Being
DPH	North Carolina Division of Public Health
LHD	local health department
NCDHHS	North Carolina Department of Health and Human Services
NCLHDA Board	North Carolina Local Health Department Accreditation Board

Chapter 1

Introduction to Public Health

What Is Public Health?

Public health is the work of promoting and protecting health at the population level. The oldest and most traditional concerns of public health are disease control and sanitation, and the public health system continues to carry out those functions today. Public health's lead role in communicable disease surveillance, prevention, and response was recently on full display during the COVID-19 pandemic. The pandemic pushed public health into the limelight, making visible the otherwise often invisible work that is constantly being carried out to make the public safer and healthier.

As the understanding of determinants of health has evolved beyond disease and sanitation alone, the public health system has expanded its focus over the centuries to include other duties and embrace additional roles. For example, public health agencies today may be responsible for monitoring trends in chronic disease and injury, administering public benefit programs, engaging in community outreach and education, operating health promotion programs, providing clinical health services, conducting research, supporting emergency preparedness and response, developing policy, and enforcing public health laws.

Public health is often associated, and sometimes conflated, with health care. Although some public health agencies provide direct clinical services, the two fields—public health and health care—are different in important ways. While health care typically involves addressing the needs of individual patients one at a time, public health is concerned with the health, safety, and well-being of entire communities. Public health's focus on the collective, rather than the individual, is part of why public health has historically been a function of government. There are private entities that engage in certain public-health-related activities—particularly research and the delivery of direct health services—but it is federal, state, territorial, local, and tribal governments that are responsible for the lion's share of public health work in the United States.

At the federal level, multiple agencies that make up the United States Public Health Service (USPHS) work to advance public health nationwide.[1] At the state level, North Carolina has a decentralized[2] public health system that is composed of two parts: (1) state-government entities led by state employees and officials who oversee statewide public health services and programs, and (2) eighty-six local health departments (LHDs), which are led by local government officials and employees who oversee public health services and programs in their counties. The Eastern Band of Cherokee Indians (EBCI), a federally recognized tribe in western North Carolina, operates its own Division of Public Health and Human Services, which serves enrolled tribal members.[3] North Carolina's public health system does not include a formal regional structure, although some state and local public health programs are coordinated by region for the purposes of emergency preparedness and response; consulting services related to environmental, child, and school health; and grant administration.

The roles and responsibilities of the federal government and the state, local, and tribal public health agencies in North Carolina are discussed further in the next sections of this chapter. The last section of this chapter explores the funding of state and local public health work within North Carolina.

The Federal Government's Roles and Responsibilities

The United States Public Health Service

The United States Department of Health and Human Services (HHS) is the cabinet-level department in the executive branch of the federal government that is tasked with protecting the health of and delivering essential human services to people in the United States.[4] HHS is also home to the United States Public Health Service (USPHS), which traces its origins to 1798, when President John Adams signed the Act for the Relief of Sick and Disabled Seamen to establish marine hospitals throughout the United States' waterways.[5]

The mission and size of the USPHS has evolved over time. Today, the USPHS is composed of eight agencies: the Centers for Disease Control and Prevention (CDC), the Agency for Toxic Substances and Disease Registry, the Agency for Healthcare Research and Quality, the National Institutes of Health, the Health Resources and Services Administration, the Indian Health Service, the Substance Abuse and Mental Health Services Administration, and the Food and Drug Administration (FDA).[6] In addition to these eight agencies, the USPHS has its own branch of the uniformed services, the Commissioned Corps, which is committed to advancing the nation's health.[7] Although the Commissioned Corps and each of the eight USPHS agencies have their own distinct missions and conduct their work in different ways, they all support the delivery of important public health services nationwide.

The CDC serves as the nation's lead public health agency and works to increase the country's health security through the control and prevention of disease.[8] The CDC conducts scientific research, tracks trends in disease and injury, engages in disease prevention and response, develops clinical guidance, provides funding, and offers technical assistance and other support to state, territorial, local, and tribal public health agencies. As part of its mission to control disease, the CDC is authorized to prevent the entry of certain communicable diseases into the United States and the spread of those diseases across state lines by detaining, medically examining, and releasing individuals arriving in the country or traveling between states who may carry such diseases.[9] The CDC may also issue federal isolation and quarantine orders pursuant to authority delegated to the CDC director by the HHS secretary.[10]

If the CDC is the nation's lead public health agency, then what do the other agencies within the USPHS do? The Agency for Toxic Substances and Disease Registry partners closely with the CDC to protect the public from exposure to hazardous substances by "responding to environmental health emergencies; investigating emerging environmental health threats; conducting research on the health impacts of hazardous waste sites; and building capabilities of and providing actionable guidance to state and local health partners."[11] The Agency for Healthcare Research and Quality is responsible for supporting and conducting research on the quality and safety of health care services.[12] Similarly, the National Institutes of Health is a research-oriented agency that focuses on medical research.[13]

Other agencies are dedicated to directly providing or supporting the delivery of health services to specific populations, including the Health Resources and Services Administration (people who are geographically isolated and economically or medically vulnerable), the Indian Health Service (American Indians and Alaskan Natives), and the Substance Abuse and Mental Health Services Administration (individuals with mental or substance use disorders and their families).[14] The FDA protects the public's health through counterterrorism work and the regulation of food, drugs, medical devices, cosmetics, tobacco products, and devices that emit radiation.[15]

Additional Federal Government Partners in Public Health

There are other departments, agencies, and offices within the federal government that also help advance public health. For example, within HHS, the Office of Population Affairs and the Centers for Medicare and Medicaid Services administer Title X grant funding for family planning services and major national health care coverage programs, respectively.[16] Outside of HHS, the United States Environmental Protection Agency is responsible for federal regulations aimed at reducing childhood lead exposures, and the United States Department of Agriculture administers the Special Supplemental Nutrition Program for Women, Infants, and Children, which provides food to low-income women, infants, and young children.[17] While these departments, agencies, and offices are not part of the USPHS, their work is part of a national framework that helps protect and promote the nation's health.

State Government's Roles and Responsibilities

In North Carolina, state-level public health work is led by the North Carolina Department of Health and Human Services and its Division of Public Health, the North Carolina Commission for Public Health, and the North Carolina Local Health Department Accreditation (NCLHDA) Board. The authority for these entities to carry out their work is primarily derived from Chapter 130A of the North Carolina General Statutes (hereinafter G.S.).

North Carolina Department of Health and Human Services and the Division of Public Health

The North Carolina Department of Health and Human Services (NCDHHS) is led by a secretary who is appointed by the governor and who oversees all the department's activities. The NCDHHS secretary is responsible for implementing and enforcing many of the state's public health laws.[18] For example, the secretary is granted a right of entry "upon the premises of any place where entry is necessary" to enforce public health laws set out in G.S. 130A and the North Carolina Administrative Code, and may seek injunctions for violations of these laws.[19] The secretary is also authorized to issue orders for the abatement of public health nuisances[20] and imminent hazards.[21]

Some of the secretary's public health duties and powers may be delegated to the North Carolina state health director, a position that is appointed by the NCDHHS secretary and that must be held by a physician licensed to practice medicine in North Carolina.[22] In addition to any delegated duties, the state health director has a slate of statutorily assigned powers and responsibilities. For example, the state health director is authorized to issue temporary orders requiring health care providers to report certain information related to communicable diseases or conditions that may present a danger to the public's health;[23] to inspect medical and other records as necessary to prevent, control, or investigate certain diseases and health hazards;[24] and to issue orders for isolation and quarantine.[25]

The Division of Public Health (DPH) is located within NCDHHS. DPH is the lead agency for state-level public health work in North Carolina. DPH is overseen by an assistant secretary for public health, who reports to the NCDHHS secretary. In the past, the positions of state health director and assistant secretary for public health were often held by the same person, but in recent years the two roles have been assigned to separate individuals. DPH is organized by sections, which are further subdivided into branches, programs, and units. DPH is responsible for a wide variety of statewide public health services and programs related to epidemiology, prevention of chronic disease and injury, oral health, public health nursing, women's and children's health, environmental health, health equity, and more. DPH is also home to the North Carolina State Center for Health Statistics, the Office of Vital Records, the State Laboratory of Public Health, and the Office of the Chief Medical Examiner.

North Carolina Commission for Public Health

The North Carolina Commission for Public Health (CPH) is the primary rulemaking body for public health in North Carolina.[26] Rulemaking is a function of the executive branch of government. Laws created by the executive branch are often referred to as "regulations" at the federal level and in other states; however, in North Carolina, these laws are called "rules" and are compiled within the North Carolina Administrative Code.[27]

Rulemaking bodies can only adopt rules that fall within the scope of authority granted to them by the legislature and must adopt all rules in compliance with the North Carolina Administrative Procedure Act.[28] State law grants CPH general authority to adopt rules to protect and promote the public's health as well as authority to adopt rules that are necessary to implement specific public health programs established under G.S. 130A.[29] State statute also gives CPH the authority to create metropolitan water districts, sanitary districts, and mosquito control districts.[30]

CPH members are appointed to serve four-year terms.[31] CPH's work is supported by DPH employees who provide subject matter expertise, assist with fiscal analyses, and offer other administrative support throughout the rulemaking process. CPH is required to hold four regular meetings per year, with the option to call special meetings as needed. One of the regular meetings must be held conjointly with the annual meeting of the North Carolina Medical Society, during which the state health director is required to deliver an annual report on the state of public health in North Carolina.[32]

North Carolina Local Health Department Accreditation Board

In North Carolina, every agency that operates as an LHD[33] must obtain and maintain accreditation by the NCLHDA Board to be eligible to receive state and federal funds.[34] The board is established within the North Carolina Institute of Public Health at the University of North Carolina at Chapel Hill and is composed of seventeen members who are appointed by the NCDHHS secretary. The seventeen-person board must include four members recommended by the North Carolina Association of County Commissioners; four members of a local BOH, as recommended by the Association of North Carolina Boards of Health; three LHD directors; three DPH employees; and three at-large members. Members serve staggered four-year terms. CPH is responsible for consulting with the NCLHDA Board and adopting rules that establish accreditation standards.[35] LHDs that have obtained accreditation must be reaccredited every four years.[36] The accreditation process and requirements are discussed further in Chapter 7.

Additional State Government Partners in Public Health

In addition to DPH, CPH, and the NCLHDA Board, many other state government entities support and contribute to statewide public health efforts. These include but are not limited to other agencies within NCDHHS, such as the Division of Child and Family Well-Being, the Division of Social Services, the Division of Health Benefits, the Office of Rural Health, and the Office of Minority Health and Health Disparities. Entities outside of NCDHHS that have a role in promoting and protecting the public health include the state's Department of Environmental Quality, Department of Agriculture, Department of Public Safety, and Department of Labor, among others.

Local Government's Roles and Responsibilities

The Local Health Department

Under North Carolina law, every county is required to provide public health services.[37] This may be done through the operation of a county health department, a district health department, a consolidated human services agency that includes public health, a public health authority, or a hospital authority.[38] These different types of agencies are captured in the general term *local health department*, or *LHD*.[39] LHDs in North Carolina serve as the boots on the ground of public health because of their direct role in administering programs and delivering public health services within the communities they serve. LHDs are often people's primary—and sometimes only—point of contact with the larger public health system. The different types of LHDs and the services they provide are described further in Chapter 2.

The Local Health Director

An LHD is led by a local health director, who is granted specific powers and responsibilities under North Carolina law. A local health director must meet the education and experience requirements set out in G.S. 130A-40[40] and must be employed full-time in the field of public health.[41] Much of a local health director's authority at the local level mirrors the state-level authority assigned to the NCDHHS secretary or the state health director. The authority granted to a local health director can be exercised only within the county or counties that are served by the LHD that the director oversees.[42]

Some of the local health director's duties and powers are broad in scope, such as the responsibilities to administer public health programs, disseminate public health information and promote good health, and advise local officials on public health matters.[43] Other responsibilities are more concrete and specific, such as hiring and dismissing department employees,[44] enforcing BOH rules,[45] entering into contracts on behalf of the department,[46] acting as the local registrar,[47] assisting in the development of and approving the jail health plan for county confinement facilities,[48] and serving as the secretary for the BOH.[49]

State law also assigns authority and responsibility for addressing certain threats to the public health to the local health director. For example, the local health director is charged with preventing, investigating, and controlling venereal disease, tuberculosis, rabies, and other diseases.[50] The local health director can also enforce immunization requirements set forth in state law;[51] can access protected records as necessary to diagnose, treat, or prevent a communicable disease or condition or to investigate an outbreak of one;[52] and can order quarantine and isolation.[53] Additionally, the local health director may order the abatement of public health nuisances[54] and imminent hazards,[55] as well as the embargo of food and drink in certain establishments.[56] These examples of local health directors' duties and powers under law are not exhaustive and local health directors may be tasked with additional responsibilities by their BOHs.

Local Health Department Staff

The number of staff employed by an LHD can vary greatly across jurisdictions, but all LHDs must satisfy the minimum staffing requirements set out in state law. Specifically, every LHD must employ a full-time local health director, a full-time public health nurse, a full-time registered environmental health specialist, and a full-time administrative assistant.[57] Every LHD is also required to ensure that the LHD has access to adequate medical consultation by a physician licensed to practice medicine in North Carolina.[58]

An LHD may also employ staff in other roles and positions to help carry out the agency's public health work, including but not limited to

- a medical director,
- a director of nursing,
- nursing staff with various areas of expertise (e.g., communicable disease and epidemiology, family planning, school nursing),
- physician assistants,
- laboratory technicians,
- a dentist,
- dental assistants,
- public health dental hygienists,
- registered dietitians,
- mental and behavioral health specialists,
- health educators,
- community health workers,
- information technology and security staff,
- billing specialists, and
- language interpreters.

LHD staff can also represent other areas of expertise, such as program administration, quality assurance, care management, animal control, industrial hygiene, legal and regulatory compliance, data analysis, and more.

The Local Board of Health

Each LHD has a governing board, which may be called a county board of health, district board of health, consolidated human services board, public health authority board, or hospital authority board.[59] For the purposes of this book, the terms *board of health* and *BOH* are used to refer to LHD governing boards, generally. A BOH is typically responsible for local rulemaking, establishing policies for the LHD, setting certain fees charged by the LHD for public health services, hiring the local health director, and more.[60] The composition, powers, and duties of different types of BOHs are discussed in detail in the remaining chapters of this book.

Additional Local Government Partners in Public Health

LHDs may work with a variety of other local government entities to carry out their mission to protect and promote the public's health. These local government partners may include the sheriff's department, county departments of social services, animal services, county and municipal leadership, local detention centers, public utilities, and others. LHDs also work closely with NCDHHS, DPH, CDC, and, for some counties in the western part of the state, the EBCI, to advance public health in their communities.

Tribal Public Health in North Carolina

The EBCI is a federally recognized tribe in western North Carolina. The EBCI owns more than 56,000 acres of land that is held in trust by the United States government and overlaps geographically with five North Carolina counties: Jackson, Swain, Cherokee, Graham, and Haywood. This area of land is called the Qualla Boundary and is home to the majority of the EBCI's approximately 13,400 enrolled tribal members.[61] The Division of Public Health and Human Services (PHHS) serves as the lead public health agency for the EBCI. The public health director is selected by the PHHS secretary.[62]

The PHHS secretary has authority to seek an injunction for violation of tribal public health laws[63] and to impose isolation and quarantine.[64] Both the PHHS secretary and the public health director are authorized to issue temporary orders requiring health care providers to report certain information related to communicable diseases or conditions that may present a danger to the public's health;[65] to inspect medical and other records as necessary to prevent, control, or investigate certain diseases and health hazards;[66] to exercise a right of entry upon the premises of any place where entry is necessary to enforce tribal public health laws;[67] and to order the abatement of public health nuisances and imminent hazards.[68]

The PHHS coordinates with NCDHHS, DPH, CDC, and LHDs in Jackson, Swain, Cherokee, Graham, and Haywood counties on various public health activities. For example, provisions of the EBCI code of ordinances establish environmental health requirements for food handling and preparation, lodging establishments, and public pools that are enforced through a collaboration by state, county, and tribal public health agencies.[69] Additionally, in 2020, NCDHHS and the Cherokee Indian Hospital Authority, the primary health system for the EBCI, partnered to establish the EBCI Tribal Option, which is a managed care program available to tribal Medicaid beneficiaries and the first of its kind in the United States.[70] These collaborations are important for promoting the health, safety, and well-being of those living on and around the Qualla Boundary.

Funding State and Local Public Health in North Carolina

Federal Funding

The federal government advances public health in many ways, but one of its most significant roles in public health is providing funding. Federal funding is distributed via grants and contracts that often require recipients to comply with federal standards and policies in exchange for funds. In this way, the federal government shapes public health at every level, even when it is not directly involved in program administration or service delivery.

Examples of federal funding of state and local public health work in North Carolina include Epidemiology and Laboratory Capacity cooperative agreement funds provided by the CDC, Medicaid funding that originates from the Centers for Medicare and Medicaid Services, Title X family planning services funding from the Office of Population Affairs, and funding for a diversity of nutrition services programs that are administered by the United States Department of Agriculture.

State and County Funding

When LHDs are the recipients of federal dollars, the funds typically flow first to DPH or DCFW (both housed within NCDHHS) and are then distributed to the local agencies. The North Carolina General Assembly also appropriates funding through the state budget and other legislation to support the work of local public health.

The distribution of funds by the state to LHDs is memorialized in the *Consolidated Agreement*, which is an annual "master" contract that NCDHHS enters with each LHD that receives funding distributed by NCDHHS.[71] The Consolidated Agreement sets out general terms and conditions that NCDHHS and LHDs must abide by, while the granular details of how various funds must be used are set out in Agreement Addenda to the Consolidated Agreement (often referred to as *AAs*). Each AA outlines the funding amount, scope of work, deliverables, performance measures, and funding guidelines or restrictions for a specific public health program or activity, such as family planning services or communicable disease control.[72] Many of the details of the AAs reflect requirements and restrictions established by the North Carolina General Assembly or the federal agency that provided the funding.

Dozens of AAs are signed alongside the Consolidated Agreement every year. There are several so-called legacy AAs, which address public health activities that have historically been funded consistently from year to year (though the amount of funding may change over time). Some AAs may relate to new funding streams, such as time-limited funding provided by a federal partner to help local public health agencies respond to an emerging health threat. Other AAs outline the terms for funding that has narrow eligibility criteria and is therefore only available to certain LHDs, such as a financial support intended solely for local public health agencies serving rural communities. This means that the total number of AAs differs from year to year and across LHDs.[73]

In late summer and early fall, NCDHHS and LHDs come together to begin reviewing the AAs for the next fiscal year. The AAs are typically finalized near the start of the following calendar year, which allows LHDs to advise their counties of the expected amount of federal and state support for local public health as counties begin their own budget processes in the spring.[74] Once the Consolidated Agreement and AAs are signed, county budgets are finalized, and a new fiscal year begins, LHDs access funds for that fiscal year by submitting reports and drawing down dollars from the state's electronic "Aid to Counties" system. Failure to comply with the terms and conditions of the Consolidated Agreement or AAs can result in an LHD's funding being limited or terminated.

In addition to federal and state dollars, LHDs receive funding through county appropriations. County financial support for local public health varies significantly across the state. According to a 2022 report by the North Carolina Institute of Medicine, in fiscal year 2019 the portion of total annual LHD expenditures that were supported by county appropriations ranged from just 7% for some departments to as much as 71% for others.[75]

LHDs may also generate their own fee-based revenue for certain services (subject to restrictions set out in state and federal laws). The authority of a BOH to approve a fee schedule for the public health services rendered by an LHD is described further in Chapter 9. LHDs may also receive reimbursements from Medicaid, Medicare, and other insurance for the health services that they provide.

Public Health Funding Challenges

Historically, public health funding has followed a boom-and-bust cycle in which public health crises trigger a surge in investments, only for those funds to be reduced again once the immediate threat has subsided. The COVID-19 pandemic provides a recent example of this funding approach. Prior to the pandemic's start in 2019, investments in public health systems across the United States had reached a relative low. During the pandemic, an influx of emergency funding was distributed to public health agencies nationwide to support rapid capacity building and bolster public health infrastructure.[76]

On May 11, 2023, the national COVID-19 public health emergency declared under the Public Health Service Act came to an end,[77] and that June, the Fiscal Responsibility Act of 2023 was signed into law. Among other things, the new law rescinded approximately $28 billion in unobligated COVID-19 funds that had been disbursed to public health agencies earlier during the pandemic.[78] In its summary of the law's impact on public health, the Congressional Research Service noted that "Several [USPHS] agencies and funded [state, local, tribal, and territorial] health agencies are likely to see a funding 'cliff' as pandemic supplemental funding ends."[79] The Congressional Research Service further observed that "Several analyses have attributed challenges in the U.S. response to the COVID-19 pandemic to inadequate or variable public health funding preceding the pandemic."[80]

Another significant challenge for public health is that funders of governmental public health work often operate independently rather than through a single, coordinated effort. Although the CDC is the nation's lead public health agency, neither the CDC nor any other specific department, agency, or office of the federal government acts as the primary coordinator of funding for state, territorial, local, and tribal public health systems. Standards for data collection, reporting timelines, and performance measures often vary between funders and even across different grants or contracts offered by the same funder. Many federal funding sources are also program- or service-specific and place strict, detailed limits on when, where, how, and by whom the funds may be expended.

Navigating the complex patchwork of public health funding is no small feat and often requires the input of significant resources and staff time by the agencies that receive these funds. The practice of allocating funding for specific activities with detailed expenditure restrictions—rather than distributing funds in a more general, flexible manner—can also make it challenging for public health agencies to deliver services and run programs that are tailored and responsive to the unique needs of their communities.

Notes

1. *Who We Are: Our Story*, Commissioned Corps of the U.S. Pub. Health Serv. (Feb. 3, 2025), https://www.usphs.gov/about-us [https://perma.cc/97JP-9VGB].
2. *General Information*, N.C. Dep't of Health & Hum. Servs. (Jan. 27, 2025), https://www.dph.ncdhhs.gov/local-health-departments/general-information [https://perma.cc/87XT-7CDY].
3. E. Band of Cherokee Indians, *Public Health Programs*, Pub. Health & Hum. Servs. (Feb. 3, 2025), https://phhs.ebci-nsn.gov/public-health/ [https://perma.cc/HX29-VJ7Y].
4. *About HHS*, Dep't of Health & Hum. Servs., https://www.hhs.gov/about/index.html (last visited Dec. 3, 2024).
5. *Disease Control and Prevention*, NIH Nat'l Lib. of Med. (Feb. 3, 2025), https://www.nlm.nih.gov/exhibition/phs_history/seamen.html [https://perma.cc/4NBS-YDGA].
6. Cong. Rsch. Serv., CRS Rep. R44916, Public Health Service Agencies: Overview and Funding (FY2016–FY2018) 2 (n.d.), https://www.everycrsreport.com/files/20170816_R44916_a55864b368ab021aef7483e36c6f4e92733a85fa.pdf.
7. *Who We Are*, Dep't of Health & Hum. Servs. (Feb. 3, 2025), https://www.usphs.gov/about-us [https://perma.cc/97JP-9VGB].
8. *Mission and Org Charts*, Ctrs. for Disease Control & Prevention (Feb. 3, 2025), https://www.cdc.gov/about/cdc/index.html [https://perma.cc/ZH9U-Q3Q3].
9. 42 C.F.R. § 70–71.
10. *Id.*; *see also* 42 U.S.C. § 264.
11. Agency for Toxic Substances & Disease Registry, U.S. Dep't of Health & Hum. Servs., *About the Agency for Toxic Substances and Disease Registry*, Agency for Toxic Substances & Disease Registry (Feb. 3, 2025), https://www.atsdr.cdc.gov/about/index.html [https://perma.cc/SML4-RU2P].
12. *Mission and Budget*, Agency for Healthcare Rsrch. & Quality (Feb. 3, 2025), https://www.ahrq.gov/cpi/about/mission/index.html [https://perma.cc/4RWN-FTLJ].
13. *Mission and Goals*, Nat'l Insts. of Health (Feb. 3, 2025), https://www.nih.gov/about-nih/what-we-do/mission-goals [https://perma.cc/7722-VRYY].
14. *About HRSA*, Health Res. & Servs. Admin. (Feb. 3, 2025), https://www.hrsa.gov/about [https://perma.cc/U5CS-CPAS]; *Agency Overview*, Indian Health Serv. (Feb. 3, 2025), https://www.ihs.gov/aboutihs/overview/ [https://perma.cc/VV2P-JNAK]; *Who We Are*, Substance Abuse & Mental Health Servs. Admin. (Feb. 3, 2025), https://www.samhsa.gov/about-us/who-we-are [https://perma.cc/FW4S-LXJZ].
15. *About FDA*, Food & Drug Admin. (Feb. 3, 2025), https://www.fda.gov/about-fda [https://perma.cc/334F-2WSQ].
16. *Title X Service Grants*, Off. of Pop. Affs. (Feb. 3, 2025), https://opa.hhs.gov/grant-programs/title-x-service-grants [https://perma.cc/7HL4-TEFH]; *About Us: Who We Are*, Ctrs. for Medicare & Medicaid Servs. (Feb. 3, 2025), https://www.cms.gov/about-cms [https://perma.cc/2ULW-D7QB].
17. *Lead Regulations*, Env't Prot. Agency (Feb. 3, 2025), https://www.epa.gov/lead/lead-regulations [https://perma.cc/CD36-BELJ]; *WIC: USDA's Special Supplemental Nutrition Program for Women, Infants, and Children*, Food & Nutrition Serv. (Feb. 3, 2025), https://www.fns.usda.gov/wic [https://perma.cc/BTX5-QMTC].
18. G.S. 130A, §§ 4, 5.
19. G.S. 130A, §§ 17–18.
20. G.S. 130A-19.
21. G.S. 130A-20.
22. G.S. 130A, §§ 3, 6.
23. G.S. 130A-141.1.

24. G.S. 130A, §§ 15(a), 144(b).
25. G.S. 130A-145.
26. G.S. 130A-29.
27. G.S. 150B-2(8a).
28. G.S. 150B.
29. G.S. 130A-29(a) to (c).
30. G.S. 130A-29(d).
31. G.S. 130A-30(b1).
32. G.S. 130A-33.
33. The statutory definition of *local health department* at G.S. 130A-2(5) includes county health departments, district health departments, and public health authorities. The definition does not mention consolidated human services agencies that include public health; however, G.S. 130A-43(a) states that such agencies "shall have the responsibility to carry out the duties of a local health department." Pursuant to S.L. 1997-502, § 12, a hospital authority that meets certain criteria may take on the responsibility of providing public health services to a county under G.S. 130A-34 and operate as a local health department. Therefore, consolidated human services agencies that include public health and hospital authorities that operate as local health departments are required to obtain and maintain accreditation by the NCLHDA Board.
34. G.S. 130A-34.4.
35. G.S. 130A-34.1(e).
36. Title 10A, Chapter 48A, Section .0205 of the North Carolina Administrative Code (hereinafter N.C.A.C.).
37. G.S. 130A-34(a).
38. G.S. 130A-34(b).
39. G.S. 130A-2(5) defines *local health department* to include "a district health department or public health authority or a county health department." The creation of consolidated human services agencies by boards of county commissioners is authorized under G.S. 153A-77(b). G.S. 130A-43 tasks consolidated human services agencies that include public health with carrying out the duties of a local health department. Under S.L. 1997-502, Section 12, a hospital authority may take on the responsibility of providing public health services to a county under G.S. 130A-34.
40. In addition to G.S. 130A-40, a pilot program established under G.S. 130A-40.1 creates a pathway for appointing a nurse as a local health director.
41. G.S. 130A-41(a).
42. G.S. 130A-41(c).
43. G.S. 130A-41(b).
44. G.S. 130A-41(b)(12). Although the local health director of a county or district health department has authority to hire and fire LHD employees, the same is not always true for a local health director working in a consolidated human services agency. In a consolidated human services agency, the power to hire staff (and the implied authority to fire staff) is held by the consolidated human services director, who may or may not also serve as the local health director, and such hiring decisions are subject to approval by the county manager. G.S. 153A-77(e)(1).
45. G.S. 130A-41(b)(2).
46. G.S. 130A-41(b)(13). This does not abrogate the authority of the BOCC.
47. G.S. 130A-94.
48. G.S. 153A-225(a).
49. G.S. 130A-35(e) (county health departments); G.S. 130A-37(f) (district health departments). In a consolidated human services agency, the consolidated human services director serves as secretary to the agency's board. G.S. 153A-77(e)(4). The consolidated human services director may or may not also serve as the local health director. *See* G.S. 153A-77(e)(9).
50. G.S. 130A-41(b).
51. G.S. 130A-41(b)(7).

52. G.S. 130A-144(b).
53. G.S. 130A-41(b)(4).
54. G.S. 130A-19.
55. G.S. 130A-20.
56. G.S. 130A-21.
57. 10A N.C.A.C. 46, § .0301.
58. *Id.*, § .0302.
59. A BOH is the governing body for a county or district LHD. A consolidated human services board is the governing body for a consolidated human services agency. There are two other local public health agency models in North Carolina, each of which also has a governing board: the public health authority and hospital authority. Because these two types of public health agency are uncommon, they are discussed separately at the end of this book, in Chapters 15 and 16, respectively.
60. G.S. 130A-39.
61. EBCI, *Our Community*, Pub. Health & Hum. Servs. Div. (Feb. 3, 2025), https://phhs.ebci-nsn.gov/our-community/ [https://perma.cc/YML5-QC4J].
62. Cherokee Code § 130-103. The full text of the ECBI's code of ordinances is available online at https://www.ebci.gov/ebci-code-of-ordinances/.
63. *Id.* § 130-201(a).
64. *Id.* § 130-910.
65. *Id.* § 130-906.
66. *Id.* § 130-110.
67. *Id.* § 130-200(a).
68. *Id.* §§ 130-202(a), -203(a).
69. *Id.* § 130-1.
70. N.C. Dep't of Health and Hum. Servs., *NCDHHS and Cherokee Indian Hospital Authority to Create First-in-Nation Indian Managed Care Entity*, N.C. Dep't of Health & Hum. Servs. (Oct. 30, 2020), https://www.ncdhhs.gov/news/press-releases/2020/10/30/ncdhhs-and-cherokee-indian-hospital-authority-create-first-nation-indian-managed-care-entity.
71. 10A N.C.A.C. 48B, § .0102(2). As an example, a copy of the Fiscal Year (FY) 2024 Consolidated Agreement can be found online at https://perma.cc/67JL-PRWE.
72. For example, please see the FY 24–25 Agreement Addendum no. 151 for family planning, available online at https://perma.cc/5VJR-EY6H.
73. *Introduction to Consolidated Agreement & Agreement Addenda: New Health Directors' Orientation*, N.C. Dep't of Health & Hum. Servs. (Jan. 21, 2024). A copy of the slides from this presentation are on file with the author.
74. *Id.*
75. N.C. Inst. of Med., Foundations of Health and Opportunity: Investing in the Future of Local Public Health in North Carolina 19 (Dec. 2022), https://nciom.org/wp-content/uploads/2022/12/FLPH-Final-Report_12.30.2022.pdf.
76. Michelle R. Smith, Lauren Weber, & Hannah Recht, *Public Health Experts Worry About Boom-Bust Cycle of Support*, KFF Health News, April 19, 2021, https://kffhealthnews.org/news/article/public-health-experts-worry-about-boom-bust-cycle-of-support/.
77. U.S. Dep't of Health & Hum. Servs., *COVID-19 Public Health Emergency*, (Feb. 3, 2025), https://www.hhs.gov/coronavirus/covid-19-public-health-emergency/index.html [https://perma.cc/A59E-LGEY].
78. U.S. House of Representatives Budget Comm., *H.R. 3746, the Fiscal Responsibility Act of 2023: Frequently Asked Questions*, House Budget Comm. (May 31, 2023), https://budget.house.gov/resources/staff-working-papers/hr-3746-the-fiscal-responsibility-act-of-2023-frequently-asked-questions.
79. Cong. Res. Serv., *Public Health Funding and the Fiscal Responsibility Act of 2023*, July 31, 2023, https://crsreports.congress.gov/product/pdf/IN/IN12208.
80. *Id.*

Chapter 2
Introduction to Local Health Departments

What Is a Local Health Department?

Under North Carolina law, every county is required to provide public health services.[1] This may be done through the operation of a county health department, a district health department, a consolidated human services agency (CHSA) that includes public health, a public health authority, or a hospital authority. These types of agencies are captured in the generic term *local health department*, or *LHD*.[2]

Each LHD is led by a director and has a governing board that may be called different names depending on the type of LHD that the board is associated with, such as a county board of health, district board of health, consolidated human services board, public health authority board, or hospital authority board.[3] For the purposes of this book, the term *local board of health*, or *BOH*, is used to refer to all of these types of boards.

There are currently eighty-six LHDs in North Carolina, serving all of the state's 100 counties. Of those eighty-six LHDs, eighty currently serve a single county and six serve a district comprising multiple counties. There is also a state-level public health agency: the Division of Public Health (DPH), located within the North Carolina Department of Health and Human Services (NCDHHS). Whereas each LHD is run by local government employees and is responsible for public health in the county or counties it serves, DPH is run by state government employees and is responsible for public health statewide. This organizational structure is called a *decentralized public health system* (by contrast, in a centralized public health system, all components of the public health system are led by the state government).[4]

While DPH provides guidance and leadership on statewide public health law, policy, and programs, LHDs bear greater responsibility for the direct delivery of public health services and program administration in their local communities. These services and programs are discussed further in the next section.

Local Public Health Services

The scope and range of local public health services are informed by state laws, contracts between LHDs and NCDHHS, and federal laws. While these laws and legal agreements serve as a starting point for understanding local public health services, they do not paint the complete picture. LHDs, often in partnership with community organizations, area health systems, and other government partners, may offer additional services based on the unique needs of their communities and the availability of funding or other resources.

North Carolina Law

The mission of North Carolina's governmental public health system is to promote and contribute to the highest level of health possible for the people of North Carolina.[5] In the furtherance of this mission, every LHD must

> ensure that the following 10 essential public health services are available and accessible to the population in each county served by the local health department:
>
> (1) Monitoring health status to identify community health problems.
> (2) Diagnosing and investigating health hazards in the community.
> (3) Informing, educating, and empowering people about health issues.
> (4) Mobilizing community partnerships to identify and solve health problems.
> (5) Developing policies and plans that support individual and community health efforts.
> (6) Enforcing laws and regulations that protect health and ensure safety.
> (7) Linking people to needed personal health care services and ensuring the provision of health care when otherwise unavailable.
> (8) Ensuring a competent public health workforce and personal health care workforce.
> (9) Evaluating effectiveness, accessibility, and quality of personal and population-based health services.
> (10) Conducting research.[6]

This set of services comes from work done by the Core Public Health Functions Steering Committee in 1994. The steering committee was convened by the assistant secretary for health for the United States Department of Health and Human Services (HHS) and included representatives from agencies within the department and other major public health organizations. It was tasked with creating a framework that would capture all of the core public health activities. The list of ten essential public health services was the product of the committee's endeavors.[7]

The list of ten essential public health services was formally adopted in North Carolina in 2012, when the legislature codified these services as the framework for

LHDs' key responsibilities.[8] The ten essential public health services are also reflected in the accreditation requirements for LHDs. Under state law, LHDs must maintain accreditation by the North Carolina Local Health Department Accreditation Board to be eligible to receive state and federal funds from NCDHHS or DPH.[9] The North Carolina Commission for Public Health, in consultation with the accreditation board, is required to adopt administrative rules that govern the accreditation process and evaluation of each LHD's capacity to provide the ten essential public health services.[10]

In addition to codifying the ten essential public health services, and separate from accreditation, the legislature authorized the Commission for Public Health to establish reasonable standards governing the nature and scope of the services provided by LHDs.[11] The standards created by the Commission for Public Health are known as the "mandated services rules."[12] The mandated services must be provided in every county in North Carolina. They are divided into two categories: (1) services that an LHD itself must provide and (2) services that can be provided through other means as long as the LHD can certify that the service is available to all individuals in the county or counties served by the LHD.

The services that an LHD must provide itself include regulation and sanitation inspections for on-site water supplies; regulation of sewage collection, treatment, and disposal; regulation and inspections of food and lodging establishments, institutions, and public swimming pools; control of communicable disease; and vital records registration. LHDs must directly provide, contract for the provision of, or certify the availability of child health, maternal health, family planning, dental public health, home health, adult health, and public health laboratory services in the county or counties served by the LHD.[13]

Finally, state statute identifies a small number of services that LHDs must provide at no cost to the person seeking care. This includes testing and counseling for sickle cell syndrome,[14] examination and treatment for tuberculosis or sexually transmitted diseases,[15] administration of certain vaccines to children in low-income families who meet specific criteria,[16] and testing and counseling for HIV.[17]

Contracts Between LHDs and NCDHHS

LHDs may be required to conduct specific activities under the terms of the *Consolidated Agreement*, a contract that LHDs enter into with NCDHHS. The Consolidated Agreement details the requirements that LHDs must satisfy as a condition of receiving certain federal, state, and other funds through NCDHHS.[18] The requirements of the Consolidated Agreement may be enforced by NCDHHS and under the accreditation rules adopted by the Commission for Public Health, which mandate compliance with the Consolidated Agreement's terms.[19]

Federal Law

LHDs may also need to perform certain activities to comply with federal law. For example, LHDs in North Carolina that provide clinical health services are usually subject to the Health Insurance Portability and Accountability Act of 1996 (HIPAA) and its implementing regulations. To comply with HIPAA, LHDs must develop and maintain numerous forms, notices, policies, and procedures for protecting, securing, and responding to requests for individuals' health information.[20] Other examples of federal legal requirements that apply to LHDs include the provision of interpreter services for individuals with limited English proficiency and making reasonable modifications to ensure that people with disabilities can access LHD programs and services.[21]

Types of Local Health Departments

North Carolina law allows for five types of LHD:

- county health departments (single county),
- district health departments (multicounty),
- CHSAs that include public health (single county),
- public health authorities (single county or multicounty), and
- hospital authorities (single county).

Any county may operate a county health department or participate in a district health department. Prior to 2012, only counties with populations greater than 425,000 could form CHSAs.[22] Today, any county with a county manager appointed under G.S. 153A-81 may provide public health services through a CHSA.[23]

North Carolina law also allows any county to operate a public health authority to provide local public health services.[24] Additionally, an uncodified state law, Session Law 1997-502, authorized counties that established hospital authority boards on or before July 1, 1997, and that met additional requirements set out in the session law, to assign those boards the powers and duties of an LHD.[25] Public health authorities and hospital authorities share many characteristics in common. Historically, however, few counties have adopted either model for an LHD. At the time of this book's publication, every county in North Carolina except one—Cabarrus County—is served instead by a county health department, district health department, or CHSA that includes public health.[26] Chapters 15 and 16 provide more information about public health authorities and hospital authorities, which are otherwise not discussed in detail in this book.

County Health Departments

A county health department is a single-county agency that provides public health services for the residents of the county. A county health department is governed by a county BOH[27] and is administered by a local health director.[28] The county BOH may be an appointed board made up of members who have been selected by the board of county commissioners (BOCC). Alternatively, the BOCC can elect to dissolve the appointed BOH, establish an advisory committee on health, and have the BOCC serve directly as the county's BOH.[29] Employees of a county health department are subject to the North Carolina State Human Resources Act.[30]

District Health Departments

A district health department is a multicounty agency that provides public health services for the residents of all the counties in the district. A district health department is governed by a district BOH[31] and is administered by a local health director.[32] The members of a district BOH are appointed by the BOCCs for each of the counties participating in the district.[33] In contrast to a county health department or CHSA, there is no option under law for the BOCC to serve directly as the BOH for a district health department. Employees of a district health department are subject to the State Human Resources Act.[34]

Counties may form a new district health department and additional counties may join an existing district health department upon agreement of the BOCCs and BOHs for each of the counties involved.[35] When a district health department is created for the first time, the existing local public health rules of the previous BOH for each of the participating counties remain in effect until amended or repealed by the new district BOH. Similarly, when a new county joins an existing district health department, the rules of that county's previous BOH will remain in effect for that county until amended or repealed by the district BOH.[36]

A county may also withdraw from a district health department. To do so, a majority of the county's BOCC members must determine that the district health department is not operating in the best health interests of their county.[37] The withdrawing county should provide prior written notice to NCDHHS of the county's intent to separate from the district health department.

If the BOCCs for all the counties served by the district health department determine that the district is not operating in the best health interests of each of their counties, then the district health department may be dissolved entirely.[38] Dissolution of a district health department requires providing prior written notice of the dissolution to NCDHHS.[39]

Withdrawal from or dissolution of a district health department cannot take effect until the end of the state fiscal year.[40] When a withdrawal or dissolution occurs, a certified public accountant or an auditor certified by the Local Government Commission distributes surplus funds to the counties according to the percentage that each of the participating counties contributed during the year.[41] Following a withdrawal from or dissolution of a district health department, any local public health rules adopted by the district BOH remain in effect in the county or counties that were previously part of the district until they are amended or repealed by the county's new BOH.[42]

Consolidated Human Services Agencies

A CHSA is a single-county agency[43] that must include at least two human services agencies. Most CHSAs in North Carolina include their counties' public health and social services agencies; however, a CHSA is not required by law to include public health and could instead provide other human services as assigned to the CHSA by the BOCC.[44] A CHSA may be created by the BOCC of a county that has a county-manager form of government.[45]

A CHSA is governed by a consolidated human services board. The CHSA's board may be an appointed board whose members have been selected by the county's BOCC, or the BOCC can elect to have the BOCC serve directly as the consolidated human services board.[46] When the BOCC decides to serve as the board for a CHSA that includes public health, the BOCC must appoint an advisory committee on health that meets the membership requirements of a county BOH.[47]

A CHSA is administered by a human services director.[48] If the CHSA includes public health and the human services director does not meet the qualifications for a local health director as set forth in G.S. 130A-40(a), then the human services director must, with the county manager's approval, designate another person who does meet those statutory requirements to serve as the local health director.[49] Employees of a CHSA are subject to county personnel policies and ordinances unless the BOCC decides to make the CHSA employees subject to the State Human Resources Act instead.[50]

Although there is not a dissolution procedure set out in statute, a county that has created a CHSA can dissolve the agency. Dissolution of a CHSA would involve administrative tasks such as dissolving the consolidated human services board and appointing new boards and directors, as applicable, for any human services agencies that had been included in the CHSA. Prior to dissolving a CHSA, a county should consider the potential effects on CHSA employees, who may be switching from an organizational model where they were subject to county personnel policies to a model in which they will be subject to the State Human Resources Act.[51] If the dissolved CHSA included public health, the county must identify another way to meet its obligation under G.S. 130A-34 to provide public health services.

Notes

1. Chapter 130A, Section 34 of the North Carolina General Statutes (hereinafter G.S.).
2. G.S. 130A-2(5) defines *local health department* to include "a district health department or public health authority or a county health department." The creation of CHSAs by boards of county commissioners is authorized under G.S. 153A-77(b). G.S. 130A-43 tasks CHSAs that include public health with carrying out the duties of an LHD. Under S.L. 1997-502, Section 12, a hospital authority that meets certain criteria may take on the responsibility of providing public health services to a county under G.S. 130A-34.
3. A board of health is the governing body for a county or district health department. A consolidated human services board is the governing body for a CHSA. There are two other types of local public health agencies in North Carolina, each of which also has a governing board: public health authorities and hospital authorities. Because these two types of public health agency are uncommon, they are discussed separately at the end of this book in Chapter 15 (public health authorities) and Chapter 16 (hospital authorities).
4. *General Information*, N.C. Dep't of Health & Hum. Servs. (Jan. 27, 2025), https://www.dph.ncdhhs.gov/local-health-departments/general-information [https://perma.cc/87XT-7CDY].
5. G.S. 130A-1.1(a).
6. G.S. 130A-1.1(b).
7. Fátima Coronado, Denise Koo, & Kristine Gebbie, *The Public Health Workforce: Moving Forward in the 21st Century*, 47 Am. J. Preventive Med. S275, S275 (2014).
8. G.S. 130A-1.1. The list was last updated in 2020. *See 10 Essential Public Health Services*, CDC.Gov, https://www.cdc.gov/public-health-gateway/php/about/index.html. At the time of publication, G.S. 130A-1.1 includes an older version of the list.
9. G.S. 130A-34.4.
10. G.S. 130A-34.1(e).
11. G.S. 130A-9.
12. 10A N.C.A.C. 46, § .0201–.0216.
13. *Id.*
14. G.S. 130A-130.
15. G.S. 130A-144(e).
16. G.S. 130A-153(a).
17. 10A N.C.A.C. 41A, § .0202(9).
18. 10A N.C.A.C. 48B, § .0102.
19. *See id.*, §§ .0804, .1306.
20. *See generally* 45 C.F.R. §§ 160, 162, 164.
21. *See, e.g.*, Exec. Order No. 13166, 65 Fed. Reg. 50121 (Aug. 11, 2000); Americans with Disabilities Act, 42 U.S.C. §§ 12131–12134.
22. S.L. 2012-126.
23. G.S. 153A-77(b).
24. G.S. 130A-45.02.
25. S.L. 1997-502, § 12.
26. This conclusion is based on voluntary self-reporting by LHDs to the UNC School of Government, which maintains a set of interactive, web-based maps showing different governance and organizational structures of local health and human services agencies across North Carolina. The interactive maps may be inaccurate if a local entity has not provided updated information about its governance and organizational structure. The maps can be accessed online at https://humanservices.sog.unc.edu/visualization-all/.

In 1997, Cabarrus County transitioned away from a county health department and established the Public Health Authority of Cabarrus County as a hospital authority under G.S. 131E, Article 2.

27. G.S. 130A-35.
28. G.S. 130A-40.
29. G.S. 130A-35(b); G.S. 153A-77(a).
30. G.S. 126-5(a)(2)c.
31. G.S. 130A-37(a).
32. G.S. 130A-40.
33. G.S. 130A-37(b).
34. G.S. 126-5(a)(2)c.
35. G.S. 130A-36(a).
36. G.S. 130A-36(b).
37. G.S. 130A-38(a).
38. *Id.*
39. G.S. 130A-38(b).
40. G.S. 130A-38(a).
41. G.S. 130A-38(c).
42. G.S. 130A-38(d).
43. North Carolina law does not contemplate the creation of multicounty CHSAs: "In the exercise of its jurisdiction over commissions, boards, and agencies, the board of county commissioners of *a county* having a county manager pursuant to G.S. 153A-81 may" create a CHSA. G.S. 153A-77(b) (emphasis added). Furthermore, the law assigns specific CHSA duties to the county manager, such as supervising the CHSA director, which would be challenging to divide among multiple county managers if a multicounty CHSA were ever created. G.S. 153A-77(b)(1).
44. G.S. 153A-77(b)(3) to (4).
45. G.S. 153A-77(b).
46. G.S. 153A-77(a), (c).
47. G.S. 153A-77(a).
48. G.S. 153A-77(e).
49. G.S. 153A-77(e)(9).
50. G.S. 153A-77(d).
51. *Id.*

Chapter 3

Introduction to Local Boards of Health

Types of Local Boards of Health

There are currently eighty-six local health departments (LHDs) in North Carolina, each of which has a governing board. The governing board may be called by different names, depending on the type of LHD[1] that the board is associated with, as follows:

- A county health department has a county board of health (BOH).
- A district health department has a district BOH.
- A consolidated human services agency (CHSA) has a consolidated human services (CHS) board, which has responsibility for public health if the CHSA includes public health.[2]
- A public health authority has a public health authority board.[3]
- A hospital authority that operates as an LHD has a hospital authority board.[4]

For the purposes of this book, the terms *board of health* and *BOH* refer collectively to all of these types of boards. The composition of the different types of BOHs varies, but in general, it includes county commissioners, health care professionals, public health professionals, and members of the general public.

The Board of County Commissioners as the BOH

County commissioners always play a role in appointing the members of their local BOH. Beyond that, in some counties the board of county commissioners (BOCC) may also elect to have the BOCC serve as the BOH. If a county provides public health services through a county health department or a CHSA, then state law permits the BOCC to adopt a resolution directly assuming the powers, responsibilities, and duties of the county BOH or CHS board (thereby effectively abolishing the appointed county BOH or CHS board).[5] North Carolina law does not provide an option for members of the BOCC to take over the role of a district BOH.

Advisory Committee on Health

If a BOCC takes over the role of a county BOH or a CHS board (for a CHSA that includes public health), then the BOCC must appoint an advisory committee on health that meets the same membership requirements as a county BOH.[6] The BOCC could appoint members from the (now abolished) county BOH or CHS board to serve on the newly created advisory committee, or it could identify an entirely new cohort of individuals to appoint to the advisory committee. Beyond requiring the creation of an advisory committee when the BOCC takes on the role of the BOH, state law is silent on how the advisory committee should operate. For example, there is no law that states how often the advisory committee must meet (or that even requires the committee to meet at all).

The role of the advisory committee is, as the name suggests, *advisory* in nature and it can be an important source of experience and expertise for county commissioners who may be less knowledgeable about public health matters. A BOCC that has assumed the role of a BOH cannot, however, rely on the advisory committee to carry out the duties and exercise the powers that are assigned by law to a BOH (and now, the BOCC). Therefore, a BOCC that is considering abolishing its existing BOH, appointing an advisory committee on health, and taking over the role of the BOH should be sure that its members understand the new powers, duties, and workload that the BOCC would inherit following this change.

Overview of the BOH's Powers and Duties

A BOH is the policy-making, rulemaking, and adjudicatory body for public health in its jurisdiction, which comprises the county or counties that are served by the BOH and the LHD. Every type of BOH may make local public health rules that apply throughout the BOH's jurisdiction. All BOHs also have limited authority to set fees for certain public health services provided by the LHD.

In some instances, the law assigns slightly different duties and responsibilities to different types of BOHs. For example, CHS boards have the same powers as county and district BOHs, except that a CHS board does not appoint the agency director. A CHS board also has powers and duties related to its oversight of other human services programs. Table 3.1 compares the powers and duties of different types of BOHs.

The BOH, BOCC, and local health director all have responsibility for the health and well-being of their county's (or counties') residents and must work together to carry out their missions. As a result, questions sometimes arise about each party's role—specifically, when is the BOH, the BOCC, or the local health director the appropriate party to exercise a power or take responsibility for an issue?

A shared understanding of each party's powers and duties under law can facilitate more harmonious, productive collaboration and help ensure that important powers are validly exercised by the correct parties. As a general rule, North Carolina public health law assigns powers and duties exclusively to one party at a time.[7] Where the

Table 3.1. Powers and Duties of Local Boards of Health

	Type of board of health		
	County	District	Consolidated human services
Adopt local public health rules	Yes[a,b]	Yes[b,c]	Yes[b,d]
Create LHD policy	Yes[a]	Yes[a]	Yes[d]
Adjudicate appeals related to local public health rules or penalties imposed by the LHD director	Yes[a]	Yes[c]	Yes[d]
Appoint the director, after consultation with the BOCC(s)	Yes[e]	Yes[e]	No[f]
Set fees for certain LHD services	Yes[g]	Yes[g]	Yes[g,h,i]
Prepare and approve the LHD budget	No[j]	Yes[j]	No[k]
Hire and fire LHD staff (other than the director)	No[l]	No[l]	No[m]
Sign contracts that legally bind the LHD	No[n]	No[n]	No[o]
Hire its own legal counsel	No[p]	Yes[q]	No[p]

Note: G.S. = North Carolina General Statutes; LHD = local health department; BOCC = board of county commissioners.

[a] G.S. 130A-35(a).
[b] G.S. 130A-39(a) to (f).
[c] G.S. 130A-37(a).
[d] G.S. 153A-77(d)(4); G.S. 130A-43.
[e] G.S. 130A-40(a).
[f] G.S. 130A-43(b)(1).
[g] G.S. 130A-39(g).
[h] G.S. 153A-77(d)(1).
[i] G.S. 130A-43(a).
[j] G.S. 159, §§ 11, 13.
[k] G.S. 153A-77(d)(7); G.S. 130A-43(b)(2).
[l] G.S. 130A-41(b)(12).
[m] G.S. 153A-77(e)(1).
[n] G.S. 130A-41(b)(13).
[o] G.S. 130A, §§ 41(b)(13), 43(a), 43(c).
[p] G.S. 153A-114.
[q] G.S. 130A-37(k).

law has assigned a power or duty to one of these three parties (the BOH, BOCC, or local health director), the other two parties typically do not have that power or that responsibility.

As an example, consider a county BOH in a county where the BOCC has not assumed the role and responsibilities of the BOH. State law grants the BOH authority to adopt local public health rules that apply throughout the county.[8] State law does not assign that same authority to the BOCC or the local health director, which means that the county BOH is the sole entity that can adopt local public health rules for the county.[9] Similarly, the county BOH is the sole party authorized by law to appoint the local health director,[10] and under state law, the BOCC appoints all eleven members of the county BOH.[11] As another example, the local health director may order quarantine or isolation, a power that cannot also be exercised by the BOCC or the BOH.[12]

Notes

1. LHDs are discussed in Chapter 2.
2. A CHSA may be composed of "any combination of commissions, boards, or agencies appointed by the board of county commissioners or acting under and pursuant to the authority of the county commissioners." G.S. 153A-77(b)(3). A CHSA may include public health but is not required to.
3. Public health authorities and their governing boards are discussed separately in Chapter 15.
4. Hospital authorities that operate as LHDs and their governing boards are discussed separately in Chapter 16.
5. G.S. 153A-77(a). A BOCC that wishes to assume the powers and duties of a county BOH or CHS board must hold a public hearing after providing thirty days' notice of the hearing and intended action, and then adopt a resolution formally assuming the powers and duties of the board. A BOCC may not assume the powers and duties of a district board of health.
6. *Id.* The requirement for an advisory committee on health applies only to counties that abolish their BOHs after January 1, 2012. This amounts to an exception for Mecklenburg County, which abolished its boards (a county BOH and, subsequently, a CHS board) before that date.
7. This is merely a general rule, and there are exceptions. For example, G.S. 130A-145 authorizes both the state health director and a local health director to issue orders for isolation and quarantine. If a situation arose in a county where an isolation or quarantine order was needed, it could be issued by the local health director for that county or by the state health director.
8. G.S. 130A-39.
9. The BOCC has a similar but not identical power under G.S. 153A-121(a) to adopt ordinances to "define, regulate, prohibit, or abate acts, omissions, or conditions detrimental to the health, safety, or welfare of its citizens and the peace and dignity of the county." BOCC ordinances passed under this statute do not apply to municipalities within the county.
10. G.S. 130A-40(a).
11. G.S. 130A-35(b) to (c).
12. G.S. 130A-145.

Chapter 4
Appointment of Board Members

The membership requirements of a local board of health (BOH) and who appoints the members varies depending on whether the board is a county, district, or consolidated human services (CHS) board. In general, BOH members include county commissioners, professionals with expertise in fields related to health care or public health, and members of the public. The board of county commissioners (BOCC) always has a role in appointing BOH members, regardless of the type of BOH.

Legal Authority to Appoint Members

County and District Boards

The BOCC appoints all members of a county BOH.[1] For a district BOH, the BOCC for each county that participates in the district appoints one of its county commissioners to the BOH. The county commissioners who have been appointed to the BOH then appoint the remaining BOH members.[2] Although not required by law, it is common practice for current county or district BOH members to provide recommendations to the BOCC when a position on the BOH needs to be filled.

Consolidated Human Services Board

When a CHS board is established for the first time, the BOCC must appoint members from a slate of nominees recommended by a nominating committee. The nominating committee is made up of existing members of the preconsolidation BOH, social services board, and area board of mental health, developmental disabilities, and substance abuse services.[3] Once the CHS board has been established, the BOCC fills future vacancies by making appointments from a list of nominees put forth by the current members of the CHS board.[4]

Appointing an Advisory Committee When the BOCC Is the BOH

State law allows a BOCC to assume the powers and duties of a county BOH or CHS board (but not a district BOH).[5] When the BOCC has taken on the role of a county

BOH or a CHS board (for a CHSA that includes public health), the BOCC must appoint an advisory committee on health that satisfies the membership requirements for a county BOH.[6] The role of the advisory committee is in its name: it may advise the BOCC when asked for input and can be an important source of expertise on public-health-related matters. However, an advisory committee cannot be tasked with exercising any powers or duties assigned to a BOH by law once the BOCC has taken over the role and responsibilities of the BOH. Although the law does not require the advisory committee to elect a chair, it may do so for the purpose of clearly identifying who will lead any of the advisory committee's meetings.

Size and Composition of Local Boards of Health

County Boards

A county BOH is composed of eleven members. State law requires that the board "reasonably reflect the population makeup of the county," but does not elaborate on how this requirement should be implemented.[7] A county BOH must include the following members:

- one physician licensed to practice medicine in North Carolina,
- one licensed dentist,
- one licensed optometrist,
- one licensed veterinarian,
- one registered nurse,
- one licensed pharmacist,
- one professional engineer,[8]
- one county commissioner, and
- three representatives of the general public.[9]

All members of the county BOH must be residents[10] of the county; however, if there is not a physician, dentist, veterinarian, registered nurse, pharmacist, or professional engineer residing in the county and available for appointment to the BOH, then the BOCC must appoint an additional representative of the general public to fill that professional's seat on the board. When there is only one professional residing in the county (e.g., only one licensed dentist), the BOCC may appoint either that person or a member of the general public. There is an exception for the optometrist seat on the BOH: in the event that there is not a licensed optometrist residing in the county and available for appointment, the BOCC may appoint a licensed optometrist who resides in another county or a member of the general public instead. When a member of the general public is appointed to fill a BOH seat otherwise designated for a professional, the member of the public can serve on the board in that seat only until the appropriate professional can be appointed.[11]

District Boards

A district BOH is composed of fifteen members, but its size may be expanded to up to eighteen members upon agreement of the BOCCs of all the counties participating in the district. This agreement to expand the size of the BOH must be memorialized by concurrent resolutions adopted by each of the BOCCs.[12] State law requires that the BOH "reasonably reflect the population makeup of the entire district," but does not elaborate on how this requirement should be implemented. The same law also requires "equitable district-wide representation" on the BOH.[13] A district BOH must include at least the following members:

- one physician licensed to practice medicine in North Carolina,
- one licensed dentist,
- one licensed optometrist,
- one licensed veterinarian,
- one registered nurse,
- one licensed pharmacist,
- one professional engineer,[14] and
- one county commissioner from each of the counties participating in the district.[15]

The statute governing a district BOH's membership requirements does not specifically require that members of the general public be appointed to the BOH; however, representatives of the general public may be appointed to the BOH to fill any remaining seats not held by the required professionals or BOCC representatives to reach a full board.

All members of the BOH must be residents of the district.[16] If there is not a physician, dentist, veterinarian, registered nurse, pharmacist, or professional engineer residing in the district and available for appointment to the BOH, then the BOCC must appoint a member of the general public. When there is only one professional residing in the district (e.g., only one licensed dentist residing in the district), then the BOCC may appoint either that person or a member of the general public. Members of the general public who are appointed to fill a BOH seat otherwise designated for one of the required professionals may serve on the BOH in that seat only until a district resident with the required professional credentials can be appointed.[17]

Consolidated Human Services Board

A CHS board may be composed of no more than twenty-five members. State law requires that the board "reasonably reflect the population makeup of the county" but does not elaborate on how this requirement should be implemented.[18] A CHS board must include the following members:

- one physician licensed to practice medicine in North Carolina;
- one physician licensed to practice medicine in North Carolina who is a psychiatrist;

- one psychologist;
- one pharmacist;
- one engineer;[19]
- one dentist;
- one optometrist;
- one veterinarian;
- one social worker;
- one registered nurse;
- one county commissioner;
- eight individuals who are public advocates, consumers of human services, or family members of the consolidated human services agency's clients, including
    - one person with a mental illness,
    - one person with a developmental disability,
    - one person in recovery from substance abuse,
    - one family member of a person with mental illness,
    - one family member of a person with a developmental disability,
    - one family member of a person with a substance-abuse problem, and
    - two consumers of other human services; and
- other persons, including members of the general public representing various occupations.[20]

All members of a CHS board must be residents of the county served by the CHSA.[21] The BOCC may appoint a single person to the CHS board to satisfy more than one of the membership requirements at a time. For example, the BOCC may appoint someone who is both a veterinarian and a family member of a person with a developmental disability to satisfy these two separate requirements for board representation.[22]

Table 4.1 summarizes the appointment authority and the membership size of each type of BOH.

Taking the Oath of Office

North Carolina law requires individuals who are "appointed to a county office"[23] or "appointed to hold any office of trust . . . in the State"[24] to take an oath of office. As appointed public officials, BOH members should take the oath of office before they begin exercising the powers of their office. In fact, acting as a public official before taking the required oath of office is a criminal offense (although prosecutions are rare) and may result in a fine and ejectment from office.[25] A list of individuals who are authorized to administer the oath of office can be found at G.S. 11-7.1. It includes

- justices, judges, magistrates, clerks, assistant clerks, and deputy clerks of the General Court of Justice;
- retired justices, judges, or clerks of the General Court of Justice;

Table 4.1. Board Size and Appointment Authority for Local Boards of Health

Type of board	No. of total members	Appointment authority
County	11	BOCC
District	15–18	Representatives from each BOCC[a]
CHS	Up to 25	
Initial members		BOCC + nominating committee[b]
New members		BOCC + CHS board[c]

Note: BOCC = board of county commissioners; CHS = consolidated human services.

[a] The BOCC for each county appoints one BOCC member to the board. That group of county commissioners appoints the remaining board members.

[b] To form the initial CHS board, a nominating committee is formed with members from the old social services board, members from the old board of health, and members from the area board of mental health, developmental disabilities, and substance abuse services. The BOCC selects the initial CHS board from the nominations submitted by that committee.

[c] The BOCC fills new vacancies on the CHS board by appointing new members from a list of nominees provided by the CHS board.

- any member of the federal judiciary;
- the secretary of state;
- notaries public;
- registers of deeds;
- any mayor of a city, town, or incorporated village;
- BOCC chairs;
- members of the General Assembly; and
- any clerk of a county, city, town, or incorporated village.

A deputy of any of the individuals listed above may also administer an oath of office.[26] An oath of office must be subscribed, which means that the oath taker must swear or affirm the oath and then sign a written copy of the oath. There is no law requiring that a BOH member take the oath of office in public or at an official meeting of a public body, such as a meeting of the BOH.

For BOH members, there are two North Carolina laws that set out oaths of office: G.S. 153A-26 (referencing the oath of office set forth in article VI, section 7 of the North Carolina Constitution) and G.S. 11-7. The oath prescribed by G.S. 153A-26 is required for "[e]ach person elected by the people or appointed to a *county* office" (emphasis added). The oath in G.S. 11-7 must be taken by "[e]very member of the General Assembly and every person elected or appointed to hold any office of trust or profit in the State." The language of the two oaths is similar, but not identical. Which oath should a BOH member take? It depends on whether the BOH is a county BOH, district BOH, or CHS board.

County Boards and Consolidated Human Services Boards

A member of a BOH that governs a county health department or a member of a CHS board is a person appointed to "a county office," which means that the member should take the oath required by G.S. 153A-26 and found in article VI of the North Carolina Constitution. The statute requires that a signed, written copy of the oath be filed with the clerk of the BOCC.[27] A county BOH or CHS board member is also a person holding an "office of trust or profit in the State."[28] So should members of a county BOH and a CHS board take the oath in G.S. 11-7 *and* the oath in article VI? Recent decisions from the North Carolina Supreme Court and the court of appeals suggest that state courts would be unlikely to find that a member of a county BOH or CHS board is disqualified for office by taking the oath in article VI but not the one in G.S. 11-7.[29] Nevertheless, for members of county BOHs or CHS boards who prefer to err on the side of caution, there appears to be no harm in taking both oaths of office. If both oaths are taken, they should both be filed with the clerk for the BOCC.[30]

District Boards

State law defines a district health department as a public authority, which is a type of special-purpose local government that is established to carry out a specific function (such as the delivery of public health services) and that operates on a multicounty basis.[31] Consequently, a seat on the governing board for a district health department is not a "county office." This means that a BOH member for a district BOH should take the oath of office in G.S. 11-7 that is required for persons "appointed to hold any office of trust or profit in the State"[32] but does not need to take the oath of office for county officials in G.S. 153A-26.

State law does not specify where a written, signed copy of the oath set out at G.S. 11-7 should be filed; however, G.S. 14-229, the statute that establishes criminal penalties for failing to properly take an oath of office, clearly requires that all oaths of office be filed *somewhere*. Although there are no statutory instructions for filing the oath found in G.S. 11-7, the record retention and disposition schedules established by the North Carolina Department of Natural and Cultural Resources offer some guidance.

The schedule developed for local health departments (LHDs) does not address oaths of office specifically; however, it does state that the schedule for LHDs should be "used in concert with the current Local Government Agencies General Records Retention and Disposition Schedule to provide full records management guidance,"[33] which instructs local government agencies to file copies of oaths of office with the municipal clerk, the clerk of the BOCC, or the clerk to the agency's governing board.[34] BOHs do not have clerks (or at least do not have clerk positions that are established and required by law). Therefore, filing a BOH member's oath of office with the clerk of the BOCC is the most reasonable option. To avoid confusion or controversy, it would be prudent for a copy of each BOH member's signed oath to be filed with the clerk for the BOCC for each of the counties served by the district health department.

The Board Chair

State law requires each BOH to annually elect a member to serve as board chair.[35] This election must not be conducted in closed session.[36] Unless the board's procedures or policies provide otherwise, the board chair should be elected by a majority vote of the board members who are currently serving on the board and are present at the meeting. Though the board chair must be elected each year, nothing in state law prohibits the same BOH member from being reelected for additional, consecutive one-year terms as chair. When the BOCC serves as the BOH, the chair is the same person who was elected as chair of the BOCC in accordance with G.S. 153A-39; there is no need (nor any legal requirement) to elect a different chair who takes over the gavel solely when the BOCC takes up public health matters.

A BOH may vote to designate another board member as vice-chair, though the board is not required to do so. The board may authorize this individual to exercise the board chair's powers and duties in the event of the chair's absence, death, resignation, or removal from office. The BOH chair's powers and duties include the following:

- The chair is authorized to call additional special meetings of the board outside of the regular quarterly meeting schedule.[37]
- At board meetings, the chair has the implied authority and responsibility to
  - preside,
  - ensure that the meetings are conducted fairly and in accordance with the board's rules of procedure,
  - recognize members who wish to speak, and
  - rule on motions and questions of procedure.

Other responsibilities of the BOH chair vary from board to board and person to person. For example, on some boards, the BOH chair functions as the board's primary spokesperson in the community or acts as a liaison between the BOH and other public bodies, such as the social services board or BOCC. On other boards, the BOH chair presides over meetings but does not act as an external spokesperson or liaison. BOH members should discuss and agree upon their expectations with respect to the chair's role and responsibilities.

Notes

1. Chapter 130A, Section 35(b) of the North Carolina General Statutes (hereinafter G.S.).
2. G.S. 130A-37(b).
3. G.S. 153A-77(c). At the time of this book's publication, the statute specifies that the area mental health board must be represented on the initial nominating committee, even though changes in the mental health system mean that mental health cannot be part of a consolidated human services agency.
4. G.S. 153A-77(c).
5. G.S. 153A-77(a).
6. G.S. 153A-77(a). The requirement to appoint an advisory board applies only to counties in which the BOCC assumes the powers and duties of the county BOH or CHS board after January 1, 2012. This amounts to an exception for Mecklenburg County, which abolished its boards (a county BOH and, subsequently, an appointed CHS board) before that date.
7. G.S. 130A-35(b).
8. See G.S. 89-3(8) for the definition of *professional engineer.*
9. G.S. 130A-35(b).
10. G.S. 130A does not define what it means to be a "resident" of a county; however, the term is generally understood to refer to a person who dwells or resides in a specified area. See *Black's Law Dictionary* for the definitions of *resident* and *residence*. For example, a person who owns a home and lives most of the year in County A, but operates a company in County B, could be considered a resident of County A but would not be a resident of County B.
11. G.S. 130A-35(b) to (c).
12. G.S. 130A-37(a).
13. G.S. 130A-37(b).
14. See G.S. 89-3(8) for the definition of *professional engineer.*
15. G.S. 130A-37(b).
16. See note 10 for discussion of *resident.*
17. G.S. 130A-37(b) to (c).
18. G.S. 153A-77(c).
19. In contrast to the statutes governing membership for a county and district BOH, the list of individuals who must be represented on a CHS board includes an "engineer" (not a *professional* engineer). However, G.S. 153A-77(c)(2) states that the CHS board must include "[e]ight persons who are *professionals*, each with qualifications in one of these categories: . . . one engineer" (emphasis added). Therefore, the person appointed to the engineer seat on a CHS board arguably needs to be a "professional engineer," which is defined at G.S. 89C-3(8).
20. G.S. 153A-77(c).
21. See note 10 for discussion of *resident.*
22. G.S. 153A-77(c).
23. G.S. 153A-26.
24. G.S. 11-7.
25. G.S. 14-229 (making action before taking an oath of office a misdemeanor and grounds for ejectment from office); G.S. 128-5 (establishing a $500 penalty and ejectment from office).
26. G.S. 11-8.
27. G.S. 153A-26.
28. G.S. 11-7.

29. *See generally*, Trey Allen, *One Oath or Two? What Is* the *Oath of Office?*, Coates' Canons: NC Loc. Gov't L. (Jan. 27, 2017) (analyzing cases on oaths of office), https://canons.sog.unc.edu/2017/01/one-oath-or-two-what-is-the-oath-of-office/.
30. G.S. 153A-26 states that the oath prescribed by this statute must be filed with the clerk of the BOCC. G.S. 11-7 does not specify where a written, signed copy of this oath should be filed; however, G.S. 14-229, the statute that establishes criminal penalties for failing to properly take an oath of office, clearly requires that all oaths of office be filed somewhere.
31. G.S. 130A-36(a). *See generally*, Kara Millonzi, *Special Purpose Governments and Public Authorities*, Coates' Canons: NC Loc. Gov't L. (Feb. 10, 2015), https://canons.sog.unc.edu/2015/02/special-purpose-local-governments-and-public-authorities/.
32. G.S. 11-7.
33. N.C. Dep't of Nat. & Cultural Res., Records Retention and Disposition Schedule: Local Health Departments 3 (Mar. 1, 2019), https://archives.ncdcr.gov/local-health-departments-schedule/open.
34. N.C. Dep't of Nat. & Cultural Res., Records Retention and Disposition Schedule, General Records Schedule: Local Government Agencies 73 (Oct. 1, 2021), https://archives.ncdcr.gov/government/local-government-agencies/general-records-schedule-local-government-agencies.
35. G.S. 130A-35(e) (county BOH); G.S. 130A-37(f) (district BOH); G.S. 153A-77(c) (CHS board).
36. G.S. 143-318.11(a)(6) (prohibiting a public body from considering the qualifications or appointment of a member during a closed session of an official meeting). The fact that a board member has been nominated to serve as chair does not disqualify the nominee from participating in the election of the board's chair.
37. G.S. 130A-35(i) (county BOH); G.S. 130A-37(j) (district BOH); G.S. 153A-77(c) (CHS board).

Chapter 5

Terms, Term Limits, and Removal of Board Members

Regular Terms and Term Limits

The length of terms and the number of consecutive terms that someone may serve on a board of health (BOH) varies by type of board. When a BOH is first appointed, members may be appointed to terms of different lengths to establish a staggered term structure. Term lengths and limits for each type of BOH are described in the following sections and summarized in Table 5.1.

County and District Boards

County and district BOH members are appointed by board(s) of county commissioners (BOCC) to three-year terms and may serve a maximum of three consecutive, three-year terms.[1] There are two exceptions to this general rule. First, if the BOH member is the only county or district resident who is a member of one of the licensed professions that must be represented on the board, the member may serve more than three consecutive three-year terms.[2] Second, the state attorney general has advised that a district BOH member who is serving in their capacity as a county commissioner may continue to serve on the BOH in a commissioner seat for as long as they remain a commissioner, even if that time exceeds three consecutive three-year terms.[3]

Table 5.1. Term Lengths and Term Limits for Members of Local Boards of Health

	Type of board	
	County or district	Consolidated human services
Length (years)	3	4
Limit (consecutive terms)	3	2

If a member of a county or district BOH vacates their position before the end of their three-year term, the person who is appointed to fill that vacancy serves for the remaining portion of the original member's three-year term.[4] State law does not establish a timeline for how quickly a vacant seat on a county or district BOH must be filled, though the BOCC should act expeditiously to ensure the vacancy does not interfere with the BOH's ability to conduct business.

Consolidated Human Services Boards

Members of consolidated human services (CHS) boards are appointed by the BOCC to four-year terms and may serve a maximum of two consecutive, four-year terms. Unlike for county and district BOHs, there is no exception to the limits on term length or consecutive terms for a member who is the only county resident licensed in a profession that must be represented on the board.[5] The county commissioner member of the board may serve in that role on the board only while that member remains a county commissioner.[6]

Removal of Board Members

Grounds for Removal

A member of an appointed BOH may be removed from office before the end of the member's term only if there is cause for removal under North Carolina law. A BOH member may be removed for

- commission of a felony or other crime involving moral turpitude;
- violation of a state law governing conflicts of interest;
- violation of a written policy adopted by the county commissioners (or by all of the applicable boards of commissioners, if it is a multicounty board);
- habitual failure to attend meetings;
- conduct that tends to bring the office into disrepute; or
- failure to maintain the qualifications for appointment (such as maintaining residency in the county or licensure in a profession).[7]

The laws governing removal of a member from a county, district, or CHS board all require that the member first be given written notice of the basis for the member's removal and an opportunity to respond to that written notice.[8]

Legal Authority to Remove a Board Member

Who has the authority to remove a member of an appointed BOH? The answer varies by type of BOH. For county BOHs and CHS boards, the BOCC has the authority to remove members. A county BOH or CHS board may recommend removal of a member to the BOCC, but it lacks power to effectuate the removal on its own.[9] For district BOHs, the BOH itself may remove a member; action by the BOCCs of the counties represented by the district is not required.[10]

Board of County Commissioners as the Board of Health

If the county commissioners have assumed the powers and duties of the BOH, a commissioner's time on the BOH ends when that person's service as a county commissioner ends. The members of a BOCC are elected by the public and state law does not provide a pathway for the BOCC to unilaterally remove one of its own members.[11]

When the BOCC serves as the BOH, the BOCC must appoint an advisory committee on health that meets the membership requirements of a county BOH. The law that requires the appointment of an advisory committee does not establish terms or term limits for the advisory committee members.[12] State law is silent as to when or why a member can be removed from an advisory committee; however, because the BOCC appoints the members of the advisory committee, the BOCC has implied authority to remove members of the advisory committee, too.

Notes

1. Chapter 130A, Sections 35(c) (county BOH) and 37(c) (district BOH) of the North Carolina General Statutes (hereinafter G.S.).
2. G.S. 130A-35(c) (county BOH); G.S. 130A-37(c) (district BOH).
3. *NCGS 130A-37; County Commissioner; District Board of Health*, Op. N.C. Att'y Gen., 1998 WL 856356 (Office of the N.C. Att'y Gen. Oct. 8, 1998). Although the attorney general's opinion addressed district boards of health, not county boards of health, some county boards of health have followed this practice as well.
4. G.S. 130A-37(d) (county BOH); G.S. 130A-37(e) (district BOH).
5. G.S. 153A-77(c). Before 2012, state law allowed only counties with populations exceeding 425,000 to form CHS boards. *See* S.L. 2012-126, § 1 (repealing the population-threshold requirement). This could explain why there is no provision for a term extension, as a consolidated human services agency was originally only allowed in counties with large populations that would be expected to have multiple eligible candidates to fill any one board seat.
6. G.S. 153A-77(c).
7. G.S. 130A-35(g) (county BOH); G.S. 130A-37(h) (district BOH); G.S. 153A-77(c) (CHS board).
8. G.S. 130A-35(g) (county BOH); G.S. 130A-37(h) (district BOH); G.S. 153A-77(c) (CHS board).
9. G.S. 130A-35(g) (county BOH); G.S. 153A-77(c) (CHS board).
10. G.S. 130A-37(h).
11. For more information about removal of elected officials, see Robert Joyce, *Removing Elected Board Members from Office*, Coates' Canons: NC Loc. Gov't L. (Feb. 4, 2015), https://canons.sog.unc.edu/2015/02/removing-elected-board-members-from-office/.
12. G.S. 153A-77(a).

Chapter 6
The Board's Responsibilities Regarding the Local Health Director

Authority to Appoint the Local Health Director

The local health director serves an important role in their community and has myriad powers and responsibilities set out in North Carolina law.[1] The entity that appoints the local health director differs based on whether the governing board for the local health department (LHD) is a county board of health (BOH), district BOH, or consolidated human services (CHS) board, and in the case of a county BOH or a CHS board, whether the board of county commissioners (BOCC) has taken on the role of the county BOH or CHS board.

County and District Boards

State law authorizes county BOHs and district BOHs to appoint the local health director after consultation with the BOCC for the county or counties served by the LHD.[2] In a county where the BOCC has assumed the powers and responsibilities of the county BOH, the BOCC appoints the local health director.[3]

Consolidated Human Services Boards

In counties with a consolidated human services agency (CHSA), the human services director is appointed by the county manager with the advice and consent of the CHS board.[4] The decision to consent to the appointment of a particular individual as CHS director will require a vote of the CHS board. As a matter of procedure, the county manager should receive consent from the CHS board prior to appointing the

---

Portions of this chapter have been adapted from Kristi A. Nickodem, *Advising, Evaluating, Disciplining, and Dismissing the Director of Social Services*, *in* Local Social Services Boards in North Carolina ch. 8 (UNC School of Government, 2023). Information specific to local boards of health and local health directors has been added, while information that applies only to social services has been removed.

director. In a county where the BOCC has assumed the powers and responsibilities of the CHS board, the BOCC consents to the appointment of the CHS director.

The CHS director or the director's designee has the same powers and duties as a local health director under G.S. 130A-41.[5] If the CHS director does not meet the qualification requirements for a local health director (discussed in the next section), then the CHS director must appoint, with the county manager's approval, an individual who does meet those requirements to serve as the local health director.[6]

Vacancies Exceeding Sixty Days

When a BOH fails to appoint a local health director within sixty days of the position becoming vacant, state law authorizes the state health director to appoint a local health director to serve until the BOH can make an appointment.[7]

Required Qualifications for the Local Health Director

Any person appointed to the position of local health director must possess one of the following:

1. a medical doctorate;
2. a master's degree in public health administration, and at least one year of employment experience in health programs or health services;
3. a master's degree in a public health discipline other than public health administration, and at least three years of employment experience in health programs or health services;
4. a master's degree in public administration, and at least two years of experience in health programs or health services;
5. a master's degree in a field related to public health, and at least three years of experience in health programs or health services; or
6. a bachelor's degree in a field related to public health and at least seven years of experience in health programs or health services, which must include at least three years of supervisory experience.[8]

Advance review and approval by the state health director is required if the BOH (or, in the case of a CHSA, the county manager or CHS director) wishes to appoint a candidate who is eligible under item 5 or 6 in the list above. When advance review is required, the BOH must send the state health director a copy of the candidate's application and any other pertinent materials. If the state health director determines that the candidate's degree is not in a field related to public health, then the state health director must notify the BOH in writing within fifteen days of receiving the candidate's application and materials. Otherwise, the candidate is considered to have satisfied the educational requirements, and may be appointed to the position of local health director.[9]

Evaluating the Local Health Director

Due to its express authority to appoint and dismiss the local health director, a county or district BOH has the implied authority and responsibility to evaluate the director's performance.[10] In a county served by a CHSA, a CHS director is appointed or dismissed by the county manager with the advice and consent of the CHS board.[11] As described above, if the CHS director does not meet the statutory requirements for a local health director set forth at G.S. 130A-40(a), then the CHS director must, with the county manager's approval, appoint an individual who does meet those requirements to serve as the local health director.[12] Alternatively, if the CHS director meets the statutory qualifications of a health director, the CHS director may serve as the local health director. Although a CHS board may be involved in the evaluation of the CHS director, the responsibility for evaluating the CHS director ultimately falls to the county manager. This section explains how a county or district BOH may evaluate a local health director (though similar processes may be used for a county manager's evaluation of the CHS director).

At the time of this book's publication, the accreditation standards for LHDs require an annual performance review of the local health director; however, state law does not provide a procedure for evaluating the local health director.[13] This means that each BOH may adopt its own policies and procedures for evaluating the local health director. However, in some counties, the human resources department may want all county employees to be evaluated using a similar evaluation tool or on a similar schedule. Since merit-based salary increases may be tied to the county's evaluation process, a county BOH should learn what the county's human resources department expects before developing an evaluation process for the local health director.

Regular evaluation of the local health director's performance is important for several reasons:

- Routine evaluations provide important feedback to the local health director about whether the director is meeting the BOH's expectations. They allow the board to review the director in a *proactive* way, as opposed to merely *reacting* to a crisis or problem.
- Routine evaluations give the BOH an opportunity to better understand the external and internal challenges that may affect the local health director's performance.
- Routine evaluations give the local health director and the BOH an opportunity to clarify areas of misunderstanding about the director's role, the BOH's role, or issues happening within the LHD.
- Routine evaluations allow the BOH to acknowledge and reward good performance.
- Routine evaluations allow the BOH to document performance concerns and how those concerns are addressed over time. If the BOH ultimately has to discipline or dismiss a local health director for performance reasons, the BOH should have documentation of its concerns that led to the discipline or dismissal.

When developing a procedure for evaluating the local health director, a BOH may want to consider the following factors and practices derived from public administration literature.[14]

Time

The BOH should devote sufficient time to planning the evaluation process, conducting each evaluation, and discussing the results with the local health director.

Criteria

The BOH should agree upon standardized evaluation criteria so that the director's performance can be measured in a consistent way from one evaluation to the next.

Frequency

The current accreditation standards for LHDs require an annual performance review of the local health director, but the BOH may choose to evaluate the director more often.[15] For example, if a newly appointed director is serving a probationary period of employment, the BOH should evaluate the director before the end of that period. The BOH may also use more frequent evaluation as part of a plan to help the director get back on track after a period of unsatisfactory performance.

Form

It may be helpful for the BOH to develop an evaluation form to capture and measure the BOH's evaluation criteria and goals for the director's performance. BOH members should also understand how their responses on individual evaluation forms will be compiled and synthesized into a final evaluation provided to the director.

Process

The BOH should develop a process to collect and discuss feedback regarding the director's performance. A common process is to ask each BOH member to evaluate the director using the standards and methods specified by the board, meet to discuss the evaluations completed by each BOH member, synthesize the evaluations into a single final evaluation, and discuss the final evaluation with the director.

The BOH's discussion of the director's performance must take place at an official meeting of the BOH but may be conducted during a closed session called pursuant to G.S. 143-318.11(a)(6). All information related to the board's evaluation of the director is part of the director's personnel record and is protected by the confidentiality requirements of state law.[16]

Flexibility

The BOH should periodically discuss, revisit, and update its evaluation process to determine what is working well and what could be improved. For example, the board may discover that certain performance criteria are unrealistic or no longer applicable. The board may find that certain evaluation questions elicit more helpful information than others. The board should be flexible, curious, and open to continuous improvement in how it evaluates the director. This may include seeking input from the director or from boards in other counties about current best practices for performance evaluations.

Director Input

As a best practice, BOHs should seek the director's input while developing the evaluation process. What are the director's own goals for the department? How does the director think progress toward those goals should be measured and evaluated? What would the director like to learn from each evaluation process? The BOH and the director can discuss these questions together when developing evaluation criteria and expectations.

Director Self-Assessment

The BOH may want to ask the director to complete a self-evaluation as part of each performance evaluation process. This allows the BOH to learn about the local health director's accomplishments, challenges, and perceptions of the director's own performance.

For a more detailed resource on developing and conducting performance evaluations, please read Vaughn Mamlin Upshaw's book, *How Are We Doing? Evaluating Manager and Board Performance* (UNC School of Government 2014). While this book is tailored toward evaluating city and county managers, it provides principles and recommendations that may also be useful in evaluating the director of an LHD.

Disciplining and Dismissing the Local Health Director

A county or district BOH has the exclusive legal authority to discipline or dismiss (terminate) the local health director.[17] When disciplining or dismissing the local health director, a county or district BOH must comply with the requirements of the State Human Resources Act (SHRA) and the rules adopted by the State Human Resources Commission (SHRC).[18] A BOH should consult with its human resources function—and legal counsel, if possible—before taking action to discipline or dismiss a local health director.

In a county served by a CHSA, the authority to discipline or dismiss the CHS director lies with the county manager, though the county manager must seek the advice and consent of the CHS board before dismissing the director.[19] If someone other than the CHS director serves as the local health director, then the CHS director is the one responsible for disciplining or dismissing that employee.[20] For purposes of this chapter, the person with legal authority to discipline or dismiss the local health director of a CHSA will hereinafter be referred to as the local health director's "supervisor."

CHSA employees, including the CHS director, are not subject to the SHRA unless the county expressly elects to keep the CHSA's employees subject to the SHRA.[21] Instead, they are subject solely to county personnel policies. **The remainder of this chapter discusses the requirements of the SHRA and SHRC rules. These requirements will not apply to the CHS director or local health director in many counties with CHSAs.**

Dismissal, Discipline, and Open Meetings Law

All discussions by the BOH regarding the local health director's performance, competence, fitness, or character or to hear or investigate any complaint, charge, or grievance by or against the director must take place at an official board meeting and during a closed session pursuant to G.S. 143-318.11(a)(6). However, if the BOH determines that the local health director should be dismissed, the final action to dismiss the director must be taken by the board in an open meeting and not during a closed session.[22]

Guidance from Human Resources or Legal Counsel

If a BOH is considering disciplining or dismissing the local health director, guidance on how to comply with SHRA and SHRC requirements should be sought from legal counsel, the human resources office for the BOH's county (or counties), the Office of State Human Resources' local government team, or a combination of the three.

Discipline and Dismissal when the Local Health Director Does Not Have Career Status

Under the SHRA and the SHRC rules, a local health director receives different protections from discipline and dismissal if the director is a "career status" employee. To attain career status, the director must be (1) in a permanent position with a permanent appointment and (2) continuously employed in a position subject to the SHRA for the immediate twelve preceding months.[23]

At any time before achieving career status, including during any probationary period, a local health director may be disciplined or dismissed for causes related to performance of duties or for personal conduct detrimental to the LHD without any right of appeal or hearing.[24] The director must be given notice of dismissal, including reasons for the dismissal.[25] It is a best practice to put such a notice in writing.

Discipline and Dismissal when the Local Health Director Has Career Status

Once the local health director attains career status under the SHRA, that individual is no longer an at-will employee and must be given due process prior to termination.[26] A local health director who has earned career status can be dismissed, suspended, or demoted for disciplinary reasons only for just cause, which includes (1) unsatisfactory job performance, or (2) unacceptable personal conduct.[27] These two categories are not mutually exclusive.[28] Certain actions by a local health director could fall into both categories. A local health director with career status who has been demoted, suspended, or dismissed for unsatisfactory job performance or unacceptable personal conduct has the right to appeal the demotion, suspension, or dismissal.[29]

Unsatisfactory job performance is defined as "work-related performance that fails to meet job requirements as specified in the job description, work plan, or as directed by the management of the work unit or agency."[30] The SHRC rules provide that this category is intended to "assist and promote improved employee performance, rather than to punish" and that discipline under the category is "intended to bring about a permanent improvement in job performance."[31]

To be dismissed for a current incident of unsatisfactory job performance, the local health director must receive at least *two* prior disciplinary actions.[32] First, the director must receive one or more written warnings. Second, the director must receive an additional written warning or other disciplinary action that notifies the director that failure to make the required performance improvements may result in dismissal.

Another basis for just-cause suspension, demotion, or dismissal is "unacceptable personal conduct," which is defined in the North Carolina Administrative Code.

> Unacceptable personal conduct means:
>
> (1) conduct on or off the job that is related to the director's job duties and responsibilities for which no reasonable person should expect to receive prior warning;
> (2) conduct that constitutes a violation of State or federal law;
> (3) conviction of a felony that is detrimental to or impacts the director's service to the agency;
> (4) the willful violation of work rules;
> (5) conduct unbecoming an employee that is detrimental to the agency's service;
> (6) the abuse of client(s), patient(s), or a person(s) over whom the director has charge or to whom the director has a responsibility, or of an animal owned or in the custody of the agency;
> (7) falsification of an employment application or other employment documentation;
> (8) insubordination that is the willful failure or refusal to carry out an order from an authorized supervisor;
> (9) absence from work after all authorized leave credits and benefits have been exhausted; or
> (10) failure to maintain or obtain credentials or certifications.[33]

Even one act of unacceptable personal conduct that falls in one of these categories may constitute just cause for discipline, up to and including dismissal.[34] Another category of unacceptable personal conduct is "grossly inefficient job performance." Grossly inefficient job performance means

> the [director] fails to perform job requirements as specified in the job description, work plan, or as directed by the management of the work unit or agency and that failure results in:
>
> (1) death or serious harm or the creation of the potential for death or serious harm, to a client(s), an employee(s), members of the public or to a person(s) over whom the [director] has responsibility; or
> (2) the loss of or damage to agency property or funds that result in a serious impact on the agency or work unit.[35]

The local health director may be dismissed for a current incident of unacceptable personal conduct (including grossly inefficient job performance) without *any* prior active disciplinary actions.[36] The BOH (or, in a CHSA, the local health director's supervisor) may impose any level of discipline—including a suspension, demotion, or dismissal—without warning if it is based on unacceptable personal conduct.[37] Prior to imposing discipline based on unacceptable personal conduct, the BOH (or in a CHSA, the local health director's supervisor) should consider the severity of the violation, the subject matter involved, the resulting harm, the director's work history, and discipline imposed in other cases involving similar violations.[38]

Forms of Discipline Other than Dismissal

Outside of dismissal, there are several disciplinary tools that may be used to course correct a local health director whose performance is not up to par, which include the following.

Written Warning

The BOH (or, in a CHSA, the local health director's supervisor) may elect to issue a written warning for grossly inefficient job performance or unacceptable personal conduct. Under the N.C. Administrative Code,

> [t]he written warning must:
>
> (1) Inform the employee [in this context, the local health director] that this is a written warning, and not some other non-disciplinary process such as counseling;
> (2) Inform the employee of the specific issues that are the basis for the warning;
> (3) Tell the employee what specific corrections, if applicable, must be made to address these specific issues;

(4) Tell the employee the time frame allowed for making the required corrections. Immediate correction is required for grossly inefficient job performance or unacceptable personal conduct;
(5) Tell the employee the consequences of failing to make the required corrections; and
(6) Tell the employee of any appeal rights provided by agency policy.[39]

Disciplinary Suspension Without Pay

The local health director may be suspended without pay (1) for disciplinary purposes for unsatisfactory job performance after the receipt of at least one prior disciplinary action, or (2) without any prior warning for causes relating to any form of unacceptable personal conduct or grossly inefficient job performance. Prior to placing the director on disciplinary suspension without pay, the BOH (or, in a CHSA, the local health director's supervisor) must conduct a pre-disciplinary conference with the director. The BOH (or, in a CHSA, the local health director's supervisor) must also provide the director with a written statement identifying the specific acts or omissions for which the director is being suspended and detailing the director's appeal rights.[40]

An investigatory leave *with* pay, which may be used to temporarily remove the director from work status in certain circumstances, does not constitute a disciplinary action.[41]

Demotion

Demotion may be based on either unsatisfactory or grossly inefficient job performance or unacceptable personal conduct.[42] The local health director may be demoted for unsatisfactory job performance after having received at least one prior disciplinary action.[43] The director may be demoted for unacceptable personal conduct (including grossly inefficient job performance) without any prior disciplinary action.[44] The director must receive written notice of the specific reasons for the demotion, as well as notice of any applicable appeal rights.[45] Prior to the decision to demote the director for disciplinary reasons, the BOH (or, in a CHSA, the local health director's supervisor) must conduct a pre-disciplinary conference with the director.[46]

Under the N.C. Administrative Code, disciplinary demotions may be accomplished in three ways:

(1) The employee may be demoted to a lower pay grade with a reduction in salary rate as long as the new salary rate does not exceed the maximum of the salary range for the new lower pay grade;
(2) The employee may be demoted to a lower pay grade without a reduction in salary rate as long as the new salary rate does not exceed the maximum of the salary rate for the new lower pay grade; or
(3) The employee may be demoted while retaining the same pay grade with a reduction in salary rate.[47]

A demoted employee's salary rate must not be reduced to less than the minimum salary rate for the applicable pay grade (for either the employee's role or the role to which the employee is being demoted).[48] If decisions regarding the director's salary must be approved by the BOCC, the BOCC must also concur in any decisions to reduce the director's salary rate.

Procedures for Disciplining or Dismissing a Local Health Director with Career Status

Before taking action to discipline or dismiss the local health director, the BOH (or, in a CHSA, the local health director's supervisor) must conduct a pre-disciplinary conference.[49] The purpose of the pre-disciplinary conference is to review the recommendation for discipline with the director, listen to and consider any information put forth by the director, and ensure that the disciplinary decision is sound and not based on misinformation or mistake.[50] The director must be given oral or written notice (as far in advance as is practical under the circumstances) of the time and location of the conference and the basis for the possible dismissal, suspension, or demotion.[51]

If the pre-disciplinary conference is being held in connection with a possible suspension or demotion, the BOH or local health director's supervisor (as applicable) must give the director written notice of the specific acts or omissions that are the reasons for the suspension or demotion.[52] If the pre-disciplinary conference involves a potential demotion, the director must also be advised of how and to what extent the demotion will affect the director's salary rate or pay grade.[53]

If the pre-disciplinary conference is being held in connection with a possible dismissal, the SHRC rules set forth some additional procedural requirements. No witnesses or attorneys are permitted to attend the conference.[54] Security personnel may be present when, in the discretion of the board, a need for security exists.[55] During the conference, the board (or, in a CHSA, the local health director's supervisor) must give the director notice of the recommendation for dismissal, including specific reasons for the proposed dismissal and a summary of the information supporting that recommendation. Though the SHRC rules allow this notice to be oral, it is a best practice to provide the notice in writing. The director must have an opportunity to respond to the proposed dismissal action and to offer information or arguments in support of the director's position. The BOH or local health director's supervisor (as applicable) must make every effort to assure that the director has a full opportunity during the conference to set forth any available information in opposition to the recommendation to dismiss. However, this opportunity does not include the option to present witnesses.[56]

After the pre-disciplinary conference, the BOH or local health director's supervisor (as applicable) must review and consider the director's response and then decide whether disciplinary action should be taken. When this review is performed by a

BOH, it must take place at an official meeting of the board but may be conducted during a closed session called pursuant to G.S. 143-318.11(a)(6). If the BOH or local health director's supervisor (as applicable) decides to suspend or demote the director, the BOH or supervisor must advise the director of any applicable appeal rights in the document affecting the demotion or suspension.[57]

The BOH or local health director's supervisor (as applicable) must deliver a written letter of dismissal to the director. This letter must contain the specific reasons for dismissal, the effective date of the dismissal, and the director's appeal rights. The letter of dismissal must be delivered to the director in person or sent by certified mail, return receipt requested, to the director's last known address. This dismissal decision must not be communicated to the director prior to the beginning of the next business day following the conclusion of the pre-dismissal conference or after the end of the second business day following the conclusion of the pre-dismissal conference.[58] In other words, the BOH or local health director's supervisor (as applicable) cannot hand the director a letter of dismissal immediately after the pre-disciplinary conference.

If the dismissal is for unsatisfactory job performance, the BOH or local health director's supervisor (as applicable) has the authority to determine the effective date of the dismissal. The effective date of the dismissal must not be earlier than when the letter of dismissal is delivered, nor may it be more than fourteen calendar days after the notice of dismissal. If the local health director has permanent status (as opposed to being in a probationary period) and is dismissed for unsatisfactory job performance, the BOH or local health director's supervisor (as applicable) may give the director up to two weeks' working notice. Alternatively, the BOH or the local health director's supervisor (as applicable) may give the director up to two weeks' pay in lieu of working notice. Importantly, the ability to give the director working notice or pay in lieu of notice is applicable only to dismissal for unsatisfactory job performance, *not* to dismissal for unacceptable personal conduct.[59]

Appealing Discipline or Dismissal of a Local Health Director with Career Status

If the BOH or local health director's supervisor (as applicable) takes action to discipline or dismiss a local health director with career status, the director has a right to appeal the decision. The steps in that appeal process are described in this section.

Local Appeal

A director with career status who has been demoted, suspended, or dismissed for unsatisfactory job performance or unacceptable personal conduct has the right to appeal the decision.[60] The director has fifteen calendar days from the date when the director receives written notice of the disciplinary action to file an appeal in accordance with any "agency grievance procedure" provided for in the applicable county-personnel ordinance or grievance policy (the "agency grievance procedure").[61] If the director does not appeal the action through the applicable agency grievance procedure within fifteen calendar days, then the director has no right to file a contested case with the Office of Administrative Hearings (OAH).[62] If the director appeals the action through the agency grievance procedure, then the decision made at the conclusion of the director's appeal through the grievance procedure constitutes the "final agency decision."[63]

Appeal to the Office of Administrative Hearings

If the local health director has completed the local agency grievance process and is not satisfied with the final agency decision, or is unable to obtain a final agency decision within ninety days from the date the grievance was filed, the director may file a petition for a contested case hearing in OAH. The director must file a petition for a contested case hearing within thirty calendar days after receiving the final agency decision and serve a copy of the petition on the board.[64] If the director files a petition with OAH, OAH will assign an administrative law judge (ALJ) to hear the case.[65] The director and the BOH or local health director's supervisor (as applicable) will be given at least fifteen days' notice of the hearing.[66]

At the hearing, the director and the BOH (or local health director's supervisor, as applicable) have the right to be represented by legal counsel; to call, examine, and cross-examine witnesses; to present evidence; and to make legal arguments to the ALJ.[67] If the director alleges that the suspension, demotion, or dismissal was without just cause, the other party—the BOH or supervisor—has the burden of proving, by a preponderance of the evidence, that it was for just cause.[68] After the hearing, the ALJ is required to issue a final decision or order that contains findings of fact and conclusions of law.[69] OAH sends a copy of the ALJ's final decision to each party.[70]

Judicial Review by Superior Court

The director may seek judicial review of the ALJ's decision by filing a petition in superior court pursuant to Article 4 of the state Administrative Procedure Act.[71] A petition for judicial review must be filed within thirty days of service of the ALJ's final decision and served on all parties to the OAH proceeding.[72] The superior court judge may reverse or modify the ALJ's decision if the judge determines that the decision was unconstitutional, exceeded statutory authority, was made upon unlawful procedure, was affected by other errors of law, was unsupported by substantial evidence, or was arbitrary, capricious, or an abuse of discretion.[73] Either party may appeal the superior court's decision to the North Carolina Court of Appeals.[74]

Investigating the Local Health Director

What if the BOH or local health director's supervisor (as applicable) has serious concerns about allegations against the director but does not yet have enough information to take disciplinary action? The director may be placed in "investigation status" with pay, which does not constitute a disciplinary action under the SHRA.[75] Investigation status is used to temporarily remove an employee from active work status in certain situations.

> It is permissible to place an employee in investigation status with pay only under the following circumstances:
>
> (1) To investigate allegations of performance or conduct deficiencies that would constitute just cause for disciplinary action;
> (2) To provide time within which to schedule and conduct a pre-disciplinary conference; or
> (3) To avoid disruption of the work place or to protect the safety of persons or property.[76]

The local health director cannot be placed on investigation status "for the purpose of delaying an administrative decision on [the director's] work status pending the resolution of a civil or criminal court matter involving [the director]."[77]

The local health director must be notified in writing of the reasons for investigatory placement no later than the second scheduled work day after the beginning of the placement. An investigatory placement with pay may last no longer than thirty calendar days without written notice of extension by the board. When an extension beyond the thirty-day period is required, the BOH or local health director's supervisor (as applicable) must advise the director in writing of the extension, the length of the extension, and the specific reasons for the extension. If no action has been taken by the end of the thirty-day period and no further extension has been imposed, the BOH or local health director's supervisor (as applicable) must either take appropriate disciplinary action on the basis of the findings upon investigation or return the director to active work status.[78]

Notes

1. *See generally, e.g.*, Chapter 130A, Sections 17–28, 41, and 144 of the North Carolina General Statutes (hereinafter G.S.).
2. G.S. 130A-40(a).
3. G.S. 153A-77(a).
4. G.S. 153A-77(e).
5. *Id.*
6. G.S. 153A-77(e)(9).
7. G.S. 130A-40.
8. G.S. 130A-40(a) (county and district health departments); G.S. 153A-77(e)(9) (CHSAs).
9. G.S. 130A-40(b).
10. G.S. 130A-40(a).
11. G.S. 153A-77(e).
12. G.S. 153A-77(e)(9).
13. Title 10A, Chapter 48B, Section .1304 of the North Carolina Administrative Code (hereinafter N.C.A.C.). The accreditation process does not require an LHD to satisfy every accreditation benchmark and, as a result, a health department could still receive accreditation even if the BOH failed to conduct an annual performance review of the local health director.
14. *See* Vaughn Mamlin Upshaw, How Are We Doing? Evaluating Manager and Board Performance (UNC School of Government 2014); *see also* Margaret S. Carlson, *"How Are We Doing?" Evaluating the Performance of the Chief Administrator*, Pop. Gov't, Winter 1994, at 24 (reprinted at https://www.sog.unc.edu/sites/default/files/articles/pghowarewe.pdf).
15. 10A N.C.A.C. 48B, § .1304. The accreditation process does not require an LHD to satisfy every accreditation benchmark, and as a result, a health department could still receive accreditation even if the BOH failed to conduct an annual performance review of the local health director.
16. G.S. 153A-98 (county BOH and CHS board). *See also* G.S. 130A-42 ("[P]ersonnel records of a district health department shall have the same protections from disclosure as county employee personnel records under G.S. 153A-98.").
17. G.S. 130A-40(a).
18. G.S. 126-5(2)c.
19. G.S. 153A-77(e).
20. G.S. 153A-77(e)(1).
21. G.S. 153A-77(d). This generally occurs in the resolution whereby the board of commissioners creates the CHSA, though the board of commissioners may elect to change whether or not CHSA employees are subject to the SHRA through a separate resolution at a later date after the CHSA is created.
22. G.S. 143-318.11(a)(6).
23. G.S. 126-1.1(a).
24. 25 N.C.A.C. 01I, § .2301(b).
25. *Id.*
26. G.S. 126-1.1, 35(a); *see also* Peace v. Emp. Sec. Comm'n of N. Carolina, 349 N.C. 315, 322 (1998).
27. 25 N.C.A.C. 01I, § .2301(c)–(d).
28. *Id.* § .2301(d).
29. *Id.* § .2310(a).

30. 25 N.C.A.C. 01I, § .2302(a).
31. *Id.* at 01I, § .2302(b); *id.* at 01J, § .0605.
32. 25 N.C.A.C. 01I, § .2302(c).
33. *Id.* § .2304(b).
34. Watlington v. Dep't of Soc. Servs. Rockingham Cnty., 261 N.C. App. 760, 768 (2018) (citing Hilliard v. N.C. Dep't of Corr., 173 N.C. App. 594, 597 (2005)).
35. 25 N.C.A.C. 01I, § .2303(a).
36. *Id.*, §§ .2304(a), .2303(b).
37. *Id.*, § .2304(a).
38. *See, e.g.*, Wetherington v. N.C. Dep't of Pub. Safety, 368 N.C. 583, 592 (2015); *see also* N.C. Off. of State Hum. Res., *The Wetherington Factors*, OSHR.NC.GOV (Jan. 2024), https://oshr.nc.gov/documents/diversity-inclusion/wetherington-factors/open.
39. 25 N.C.A.C. 01I, § .2305.
40. *Id.* § .2306(a).
41. *Id.* § .2309(c).
42. *Id.* § .2307(a).
43. *Id.* § .2307(a)(1).
44. *Id.* § .2307(a)(2)–(3).
45. *Id.* § .2307(a)(1).
46. *Id.* § .2307(c).
47. *Id.* § .2307(b).
48. *Id.* § .2307(b)(3).
49. *Id.* § .2308.
50. *Id.* § .2308(4)(d).
51. *Id.* § .2308.
52. *Id.* § .2308(2)(c), (3)(d).
53. *Id.* § .2308(3)(e).
54. *Id.* § .2308(4)(d)–(e).
55. *Id.* § .2308(4)(d).
56. *Id.* § .2308(4)(e).
57. *Id.* § .2308(2)(d), (3)(f).
58. *Id.* § .2308(4)(f).
59. *See id.* § .2308(4)(g).
60. *Id.* § .2310(a).
61. G.S. 126-35; 25 N.C.A.C. 01I, § .2310(a).
62. 25 N.C.A.C. 01I, § .2310(a).
63. *Id.* § .2310(b).
64. G.S. 126-35; 25 N.C.A.C. 01I, § .2310(d).
65. G.S. 150B-32.
66. G.S. 150B-23(b).
67. *See* G.S. 150B-25; G.S. 150B-27 (subpoenas); G.S. 150B-28 (discovery); G.S. 150B-29 (rules of evidence).
68. G.S. 150B-25.1.
69. G.S. 150B-34.
70. G.S. 150B-37.
71. G.S. 150B, §§ 43, 45.
72. G.S. 150B, §§ 45–46.
73. G.S. 150B-51.
74. G.S. 150B-52.
75. 25 N.C.A.C. 01I, § .2309(c).
76. *Id.*
77. *Id.*
78. *Id.*

Chapter 7
Accreditation

North Carolina law requires that every local health department (LHD) obtain and maintain accreditation as a condition of its eligibility to receive state and federal funds.[1] LHDs that have obtained accreditation must be reaccredited every four years.[2] Accreditation helps standardize and support equality in the public health services that are provided by LHDs to communities across the state.

The accreditation process is managed by the North Carolina Local Health Department Accreditation (NCLHDA) Board. The NCLHDA Board is established within the North Carolina Institute of Public Health at the University of North Carolina at Chapel Hill and is composed of seventeen members who are appointed by the secretary of the North Carolina Department of Health and Human Services. The seventeen-person board must include four members recommended by the North Carolina Association of County Commissioners, four members of a local board of health (BOH) as recommended by the Association of North Carolina Boards of Health, three LHD directors, three employees of the North Carolina Division of Public Health, and three at-large members.[3] Members serve staggered four-year terms.[4]

The Accreditation Process

The North Carolina Commission for Public Health is responsible for consulting with the NCLHDA Board and adopting administrative rules that establish standards for accreditation.[5] The accreditation process involves a self-assessment by the LHD using the Health Department Self-Assessment Instrument and a site visit to the LHD's premises and facilities to assess whether the LHD has sufficiently met the accreditation requirements. After the self-assessment and the site visit, the NCLHDA Board issues a decision on the LHD's accreditation status.[6] The NCLHDA Board has provided detailed guidance on the accreditation process and standards in the "Health Department Self-Assessment Instrument (HDSAI) Interpretation Document," which is published on the board's website.[7]

To be accredited, an LHD must satisfy a minimum number of the accreditation requirements (but not necessarily all of them).[8] An LHD that has satisfied enough of the accreditation standards is assigned the status of "accredited" (if it is the LHD's first time undergoing accreditation) or "reaccredited" (if the LHD has undergone accreditation before). "Accredited" and "reaccredited" status is in effect for four years until the LHD must apply for accreditation again.[9] But what happens to an LHD that does *not* meet the accreditation standards? In these situations, the NCLHDA Board assigns the LHD the status of "conditionally accredited," which means that the LHD is granted short-term accreditation subject to any conditions identified in writing by the NCLHDA Board.[10] An LHD may operate as conditionally accredited for up to two years. During that two-year period, the LHD may seek to demonstrate that the conditions set by the NCLHDA Board have been met and request to be granted accredited or reaccredited status. If the NCLHDA Board determines that the conditions it set have been met, then the request is granted. The LHD's status as accredited or reaccredited is in effect for four years from when the status of conditionally accredited was assigned.[11]

If, after two years of being conditionally accredited, the LHD has not satisfied the conditions identified by the NCLHDA Board, then the LHD is assigned the status of "unaccredited."[12] The NCLHDA Board must provide the LHD and the secretary of the North Carolina Department of Health and Human Services with written notice of the LHD's unaccredited status.[13] State law requires an LHD to maintain accreditation to be eligible to receive state and federal public health funding from the North Carolina Division of Public Health; therefore, an LHD that is assigned unaccredited status is at risk of losing access to key funding streams.[14]

The Role of the BOH in Accreditation

At the time of publication of this book, the accreditation rules assign various responsibilities to the LHD and local health director related to supporting and providing information to the BOH.[15] The BOH should work with the local health director and LHD staff to prepare for the accreditation process and determine how satisfaction of any requirements related to the BOH can be best documented and presented. When the board of county commissioners has assumed the role of the BOH, it is responsible for satisfying any accreditation requirements related to BOHs.

Anticipated Changes to the Accreditation Administrative Rules

In 2013, the state legislature established a process called Periodic Review and Expiration of Existing Rules (colloquially referred to as *periodic review* or *readoption*).[16] The periodic review process requires North Carolina rulemaking bodies, including the Commission for Public Health, to review and either repeal or readopt all their rules in the North Carolina Administrative Code. Periodic review occurs every ten years. The first round of periodic review began in 2014, and the second round began in 2024.[17]

It is possible that changes, big or small, will be made to the accreditation rules during the readoption process. LHDs and BOHs that are preparing for the accreditation process should review the most current versions of the accreditation rules and the HDSAI Interpretation Document to ensure they accurately understand the accreditation requirements.

Notes

1. Chapter 130A, Section 34.4 of the North Carolina General Statutes (hereinafter G.S.).
2. Title 10A, Chapter 48A, Section .0205 of the North Carolina Administrative Code (hereinafter N.C.A.C.).
3. G.S. 130A-34.1(a).
4. G.S. 130A-34.1(b).
5. G.S. 130A-34.1. The accreditation rules may be found at 10A N.C.A.C. 48B.
6. G.S. 130A-34.1(e)(1).
7. The HDSAI Interpretation Document is updated regularly and is available on the NCLHDA Board website. *See generally*, N.C. LOC. HEALTH DEP'T ACCREDITATION, https://nclhdaccreditation.unc.edu/ (last visited Apr. 23, 2025).
8. 10A N.C.A.C. 48B, § .0103(a).
9. G.S. 130A-34.1(d)(1).
10. G.S. 130A-34.1(d)(2), (g)(2).
11. G.S. 130A-34.1(g)(2).
12. G.S. 130A-34.1(d)(2).
13. G.S. 130A-34.1(i).
14. G.S. 130A-34.4(a).
15. *E.g.*, 10A N.C.A.C. 48B, § .0601(3), (4).
16. S.L. 2013-413.
17. G.S. 150B-21.3A(c).

Chapter 8
Rulemaking

What Are Rules?

At the state level, the North Carolina Commission for Public Health (CPH) is the primary rulemaking body responsible for promulgating public health rules.[1] CPH rules are regulations that carry the weight of law and apply statewide, in every county and municipality. At the local level, a local board of health (BOH) has the authority to adopt rules necessary to protect and promote the public health.[2] A BOH rule applies only throughout the county or counties that the BOH serves (referred to as the BOH's *jurisdiction*).[3]

Like CPH rules, BOH rules carry the weight of law. BOH rules can be enforced using various methods set forth in North Carolina's public health statutes, such as a criminal charge (typically a misdemeanor), a civil action, or, in limited cases, the imposition of administrative penalties.[4] In a county where the board of county commissioners (BOCC) acts as the BOH, violation of a local public health rule adopted by the BOCC that triggers a civil penalty will not also result in a misdemeanor charge unless the rule specifically states that violation of the rule is a misdemeanor offense.[5]

If a BOH seeks to adopt a rule addressing an area of public health that is already regulated by CPH, then certain criteria set out in statute must be met.[6] There are also areas of public health that cannot be regulated under BOH rules.[7] Both types of limitation on BOH rulemaking authority are discussed in the next section.

BOH Rulemaking Authority

A BOH's rulemaking actions cannot exceed the scope of the authority granted to the BOH by the state legislature. The North Carolina General Assembly has authorized BOHs to adopt rules as necessary to protect and promote the public's health.[8] The scope of BOH rulemaking authority was interpreted by the North Carolina Court of Appeals in a 1996 case, *City of Roanoke Rapids v. Peedin.*[9] The *Peedin* decision established a five-part test that a BOH rule must satisfy to be lawful and valid. To succeed under this test, a BOH rule

1. must be related to the promotion or protection of health;
2. must be reasonable in light of the health risk addressed;
3. must not violate any law or constitutional provision;
4. must not be discriminatory; and
5. must not make any distinctions based on policy concerns traditionally reserved for legislative bodies.[10]

Express Preemption: Statutory Limitations on BOH Rulemaking Authority

Several North Carolina laws impose additional limits on a BOH's rulemaking authority. The same state statute that gives BOHs their rulemaking authority imposes two limitations on boards. First, it prohibits a BOH from adopting rules related to the issuing of sanitation grades and of operating permits for food and lodging facilities.[11] Second, it provides that a BOH must obtain approval from the North Carolina Department of Health and Human Services (NCDHHS) before adopting local rules that govern on-site wastewater management. To approve rules governing local on-site wastewater management, NCDHHS must find that the local rules are at least as stringent as the state-level rules promulgated by CPH and that they are both necessary and sufficient to safeguard the public health.[12]

Another statute addresses local BOH rules that restrict smoking in public places.[13] A BOH may adopt a rule restricting or prohibiting smoking that is stricter than state law and that applies in local government buildings, on local government grounds, in local government vehicles, or in the enclosed areas of public places.[14] Local BOH rules may not, however, restrict smoking in private residences or vehicles, nor may they regulate certain other public places specified in the law. A BOH rule restricting smoking must also be approved by the board (or boards) of county commissioners (BOCC).[15]

Implied Preemption of a BOH Rule by State Law

If a BOH adopts a rule governing an issue that is already addressed in state law, then the local rule may be preempted (overridden) by the state law. This limitation is sometimes referred to as *implied preemption*, or preemption that may be implied even in the absence of a clear statutory limitation (such as the limitations discussed in the section above). In the 2002 case *Craig v. County of Chatham*, the North Carolina Supreme Court held that a BOH rule may be preempted by state law if the state has already provided "a complete and integrated regulatory scheme" in the area addressed by the local rule.[16] However, the North Carolina statute that gives BOHs their rulemaking authority also specifically says that a BOH may adopt a rule that is more stringent than state rules if the BOH determines that the more stringent rule is necessary to protect the public health.[17]

What does this mean for BOHs and rulemaking? The court's decision does not outright preclude a BOH from adopting a rule regulating an issue already addressed in state law and implementing more stringent standards. However, to do so, the BOH must be able to provide a rationale for why higher local standards are needed to protect the public health. One way to justify the need for such a rule is to demonstrate that conditions in the BOH's jurisdiction are different from the rest of the state in a manner or to a degree that warrants the creation of a local rule with more stringent standards.

Board of Health Rule Versus Local Ordinance

A BOCC and a municipal board both have ordinance-making authority, including the authority to adopt ordinances addressing certain public health issues within their jurisdictions.[18] There are important differences between a BOH rule and a local ordinance adopted by the BOCC or municipal board, which are described in the sections below.

Territorial Jurisdiction

A major difference between BOH rules and local ordinances is their territorial jurisdiction. County ordinances apply only in the unincorporated areas of the county and not inside any municipalities (unless the municipalities consent to be governed by the county ordinance).[19] Similarly, municipal ordinances typically apply only within the municipality.[20] In contrast, a BOH rule applies throughout the board's territorial jurisdiction, which is all of the county or counties represented by the BOH, including any municipalities contained therein.[21]

Scope of Authority

Another key difference is that BOHs are subject to certain limits on their rulemaking authority that do not apply to elected BOCCs when adopting an ordinance. These limitations were described briefly earlier in this chapter, but two are worth further elaboration here. First, BOHs may only adopt rules that are related to the protection and promotion of health, whereas BOCCs are authorized to adopt ordinances that address a wider range of issues and concerns.[22] The second and perhaps more significant limitation is that a BOH must not "make distinctions based upon policy concerns traditionally reserved for legislative bodies."[23]

How do these differing scopes of authority play out on the ground? A BOCC may make distinctions based on policy concerns having nothing to do with public health. For example, a BOCC may enact an ordinance imposing certain general requirements on businesses in the community but exempting small businesses for whom compliance with those requirements might pose economic hardship. In contrast, a BOH may not craft exceptions that are based on businesses' economic concerns and that lack a health-based rationale.

Enforcement

A final significant difference between BOH rules and local ordinances is in how they are enforced. BOH rules are enforced using the specific remedies set forth in North Carolina's public health laws, such as a criminal charge, a civil action, or (in limited circumstances) the imposition of administrative penalties by the local health director.[24] Ordinances may be enforced using similar methods, but in general a BOCC has broader authority than a local health director to impose administrative penalties for local violations, as well as the option to make violation of an ordinance an infraction.[25]

BOH Rulemaking Process

Before Beginning the Process

Before a BOH undertakes the rulemaking process to adopt a new rule, the BOH should consider the following:

- Why is this rule necessary? Are there state statutes or state administrative rules that already address this issue? Are there local BOH rules or local ordinances that already address this issue?
- Does the BOH have legal authority to adopt the rule?
- Is approval by another party required to adopt the rule?
    - Does the rule regulate on-site wastewater management and therefore require approval by NCDHHS?[26]
    - Does the rule regulate smoking in public spaces and therefore require approval by the BOCC?[27]
- Who is affected by the rule? Should stakeholders be consulted on the language of the rule and if so, which stakeholders?
- What is the enforcement mechanism for the rule (e.g., a misdemeanor charge, an administrative penalty, etc.)? Does the enforcement mechanism allow local government to effectively respond to a violation of the rule and achieve the desired public health outcome?
- Once drafted, is the language of the rule clear and unambiguous?
    - Are important terms defined?
    - Does the rule specify an effective date (if different from the expected date of adoption)?
    - Is the rule clear about how timeframes for any deadlines are counted (e.g., counting business versus calendar days)?

The BOH should consider similar questions when it seeks to amend or repeal a rule. Once a BOH has decided to move forward with adopting, amending, or repealing a rule, the BOH must follow the rulemaking process set out in state law and described in the following sections.[28]

At Least Ten Days Before Rulemaking Action

At least ten days before any BOH rule is adopted, amended, or repealed, the notice of the BOH's intended rulemaking action must be published in a newspaper "having general circulation" in the area served by the BOH.[29] The notice must describe the subjects and issues addressed by the proposed rulemaking action, the proposed effective date of the rule, and a statement that copies of the proposed rule can be accessed at the local health department.[30] There is no requirement that the notice or a copy of the rule be posted on the BOH's or local health department's website, and posting on these groups' websites cannot be done in lieu of publishing the newspaper notice.

Additionally, and also at least ten days prior to rulemaking action being taken, a copy of the proposed rule must be made available in the county clerk's office. A district BOH must therefore file copies of the proposed rule with the office of the county clerk in every county served by the BOH.[31]

Meeting to Take Rulemaking Action

The BOH may vote to adopt, amend, or repeal a local rule at a regular or special meeting of the BOH. The BOH meeting must be properly noticed in accordance with North Carolina's open meeting laws (discussed further in Chapter 12), even if the BOH's only action item is to vote on the rule.

After Taking Rulemaking Action

A BOH's adoption, amendment, or repeal of a rule is effective immediately unless the rule itself specifies a delayed effective date. A copy of the rule must be filed with and maintained by the secretary to the BOH, a position that is held by the local health director (or, in the case of a consolidated human services agency, by the consolidated human services director).[32] If the BOH adopted any materials by reference in its rule, then a copy of those materials must be filed with the BOH secretary alongside a copy of the rule text.[33] Finally, the BOH should confirm with NCDHHS whether it is required by the Consolidated Agreement to provide a copy of any adopted, amended, or repealed rules to NCDHHS.

Notes

1. Chapter 130A, Section 29, of the North Carolina General Statutes (hereinafter G.S.).
2. G.S. 130A-39(a).
3. G.S. 130A-39(c).
4. *E.g.*, G.S. 130A, §§ 17, 18, 22(h), 22(h1), 25(a).
5. G.S. 153A-77(a).
6. G.S. 130A-39(b).
7. *Id.*
8. G.S. 130A-39(a).
9. 124 N.C. App. 578 (1996).
10. *Id.* at 587.
11. G.S. 130A-39(b).
12. G.S. 130A §§ 39(b), 335(c).
13. G.S. 130A-498.
14. G.S. 130A-498(a); *see also* G.S. 130A-492 (defining *public place* and local government buildings, grounds, and vehicles).
15. G.S. 130A-498.
16. Craig v. County of Chatham, 356 N.C. 40, 45 (2002) (quoting G.S. 160A-74(b)(5)).
17. G.S. 130A-39(b).
18. G.S. 153A-121(a); G.S. 160A-174(a).
19. G.S. 153A-122.
20. G.S. 160A-174(a).
21. G.S. 130A-39(c).
22. G.S. 130A-39(a); G.S. 153A-121(a).
23. City of Roanoke Rapids v. Peedin, 124 N.C. App. 578, 587 (1996).
24. *E.g.*, G.S. 130A §§ 17, 18, 22(h), 22(h1), 25(a).
25. G.S. 153A-123(a).
26. G.S. 130A-39(b).
27. G.S. 130A-498(a).
28. *See* G.S. 130A-39(d) to (f).
29. G.S. 130A-39(d).
30. *Id.*
31. *Id.*
32. G.S. 130A, §§ 39(e), 35(e), 37(f); G.S. 153A-77(e)(4).
33. G.S. 130A-39(f).

Chapter 9
Setting Fees

Authority to Set Fees

North Carolina law authorizes all local boards of health (BOHs) to set fees that are charged by their local health departments (LHDs) for certain public health services. However, there are several limitations to a BOH's fee-setting authority. County and district BOHs and consolidated human services boards must base their fees on a plan proposed by the local health director, and any fees adopted by these boards must also be approved by the affected county's board of county commissioners.[1] Fees that are set by the BOH and collected by the LHD must typically be used to support the LHD's public health programs and expended in accordance with the Local Government Budget and Fiscal Control Act.[2] Additional limits on a BOH's authority to set fees are described in the next sections.

Limitations on Setting Fees

Environmental Health Services

Generally, the BOH may not set (and the LHD may not charge) fees for activities carried out by an LHD employee acting as an agent of the state. This includes most LHD environmental health programs, which are typically led by LHD employees who are authorized by law to enforce rules promulgated by the North Carolina Commission for Public Health.[3] However, there are four areas of environmental health services where a BOH may set (and the LHD may charge) "cost-related" fees: the regulation of on-site wastewater treatment, public swimming pools, tattoo shops, and drinking water wells.[4] North Carolina's public health laws do not define *cost-related*, but such fees should be based on a calculation of the actual cost incurred by the LHD for providing the service. The calculation could include variables such as staff time and the cost of materials or other resources that are needed to provide the service.

Services That Must Be Provided at No Cost to Recipients

Various North Carolina public health laws require that LHDs provide specific health services at no cost to the person receiving the service. As a result, the BOH cannot set a fee for these services that would be charged by the LHD to the service recipient. The services that must be provided free of charge to the recipient include

- testing and counseling for sickle cell syndrome[5]
- examination and treatment for tuberculosis,[6]
- examination and treatment for certain sexually transmitted diseases,[7] and
- testing and counseling for HIV.[8]

In addition, immunizations that are required by law and supplied by the state must be provided at no cost to uninsured or underinsured patients who meet certain income criteria.[9]

Other Limitations on Fees

While LHDs may charge fees for some of their clinical services, the BOH often has limited discretion in setting these fees. Fees for clinical services may reflect Medicaid reimbursement rates or sliding scales established by a state or federal program that provides funds for a particular service. Fees may also be capped or limited by state and federal laws. For example, Title VI of the federal Civil Rights Act of 1964 prohibits recipients of federal financial assistance from charging their limited-English-proficient clients for interpretation services.[10] Similarly, a North Carolina law and the federal HIPAA Privacy Rule limit the fees that may be charged for providing patients with copies of their own medical records.[11]

Notes

1. Chapter 130A, Section 39(g) of the North Carolina General Statutes (hereinafter G.S.).
2. *Id.*
3. G.S. 130A-4(b).
4. G.S. 130A-39(g).
5. G.S. 130A-130.
6. G.S. 130A-144(e).
7. *Id.*
8. Title 10A, Chapter 48A, Section .0202(9) of the North Carolina Administrative Code. This rule allows third-party payers (such as insurance) to be billed for HIV testing and counseling services only when the patient provides written consent.
9. G.S. 130A-153(a).
10. Civil Rights Act of 1964, 42 U.S.C. § 2000d to d-7; *see also* Exec. Order No. 13166, 65 Fed. Reg. 50121 (Aug. 11, 2000).
11. G.S. 90-411; 45 C.F.R. 164.524(c)(4).

Chapter 10
Board Adjudications

What Is an Adjudication?

In limited circumstances, a person who is aggrieved by the enforcement of a board of health (BOH) rule or imposition of administrative penalties by the local health director may appeal the enforcement action or penalty to the BOH.[1] When the BOH hears evidence and makes a determination on whether the enforcement action or administrative penalty was appropriate, the BOH is conducting an adjudication. A BOH adjudication may also be referred to as a *quasi-judicial hearing* because the BOH is acting somewhat ("quasi") like a court ("judicial") when it hears and decides the case.[2]

When May a BOH Adjudication Be Sought?

Subject Matter Jurisdiction

A BOH's authority to conduct an adjudication is established at Chapter 130A, Section 24(b) of the North Carolina General Statutes (hereinafter G.S.). Adjudications cannot be used to handle any and all public complaints: the law authorizes the BOH to adjudicate only issues involving the enforcement of BOH rules or concerning the imposition of administrative penalties by the local health director. This may be referred to as the BOH's area of *subject matter jurisdiction*.[3] A BOH does not have subject matter jurisdiction to hear complaints regarding actions taken by local health department (LHD) employees to enforce statewide rules promulgated by the North Carolina Commission for Public Health; instead, those cases are heard by the North Carolina Office of Administrative Hearings.[4]

The author would like to thank Legal Research Associate Caitlin Little and Senior Legal Research Associate Alex Phipps for their assistance researching adjudications and policies of local boards of health.

Aggrieved Persons

The law governing BOH adjudications allows only an "aggrieved person" to appeal enforcement of a BOH rule or imposition of an administrative penalty by the local health director to the BOH. The term *aggrieved person* is not defined under North Carolina's public health laws. The North Carolina Supreme Court has taken the following approach to assessing who counts as an aggrieved person:

> The expression "person aggrieved" has no technical meaning. What it means depends on the circumstances involved. It has been variously defined: "Adversely or injuriously affected; damnified, having a grievance, having suffered a loss or injury, or injured; also having cause for complaint. More specifically the word(s) may be employed meaning adversely affected in respect of legal rights, or suffering from an infringement or denial of legal rights."[5]

A person who qualifies as an aggrieved person and is therefore eligible to appeal an issue to the BOH for adjudication may be described as having *legal standing*. By contrast, a member of the public who hears about an enforcement action or administrative penalty and simply thinks it unfair, but who was not otherwise affected by the action or penalty, would not likely have the legal standing necessary to appeal the enforcement action or administrative penalty to the BOH.

Statute of Limitations

An aggrieved person has a limited window for appealing an enforcement action or administrative penalty by seeking an adjudication by the BOH. This limitation on when an aggrieved person can seek an appeal may be called the *statute of limitations*. The statute of limitations for seeking an adjudication is thirty days after the enforcement action at issue was taken or after the administrative penalty at issue was imposed.[6]

Exhaustion of Administrative Remedies

The BOH adjudication process includes a final step that allows a party to appeal a BOH decision to district court; however, an aggrieved person seeking to appeal an enforcement action or administrative penalty cannot skip over the BOH adjudication process and go straight to district court. The North Carolina Supreme Court has ruled that "where the legislature has provided by statute an effective administrative remedy, that remedy is exclusive and its relief must be exhausted before recourse may be had to the courts."[7] This means that aggrieved persons seeking to appeal enforcement of a BOH rule or imposition of an administrative penalty by the local health director must exhaust their administrative remedies—that is, go through the full BOH adjudication process—before bringing their claims before district court.

The BOH Adjudication Process

The adjudication process is set out in G.S. 130A-24(b)–(d). The process involves various deadlines and quick turnarounds. BOHs are therefore encouraged to consult with legal counsel to ensure that the deadlines for the adjudication process are met and that all required components of the adjudication process are carried out correctly.

Written Notice of Appeal by the Aggrieved Person

A BOH adjudication may be initiated by an aggrieved person seeking to appeal the LHD's enforcement of BOH rules or imposition of an administrative penalty by the local health director. First, the aggrieved person must provide written notice of the appeal to the local health director. The written notice must be given to the local health director no later than thirty days after the enforcement action at issue was taken or after the administrative penalty at issue was imposed. The notice of appeal must include the following information: the name and address of the aggrieved person, a description of the challenged action (the enforcement action or administrative penalty at issue), and a statement of why the aggrieved person believes that the challenged action was improper.[8]

Transmission of the Notice of Appeal by the Local Health Director

Once the notice of appeal has been given to the local health director, the local health director has five business days to send the notice of appeal to the BOH. The local health director must also send the BOH any documents or other materials that informed the challenged action within the same five-day timeframe.[9]

Noticing the BOH Adjudication Hearing

The BOH has fifteen days from when it receives the notice of appeal and any related documents or materials from the local health director to hold an adjudication hearing. The BOH must also satisfy two notice requirements related to the hearing: providing notice of the hearing to the aggrieved person and providing notice of the hearing in accordance with North Carolina's laws regarding open meetings. The BOH must give the aggrieved person at least ten days' notice of the date, time, and place of the hearing.[10] The law does not require that the BOH give this notice in writing, although written notice (in contrast to verbal notice) has the benefit of helping memorialize that the notice requirement was satisfied.

A BOH meets the statutory definition of a "public body" that is required to make its "official meetings" open to the public.[11] The adjudication hearing should therefore occur during a special or regular BOH meeting for which notice has been properly given in accordance with North Carolina's open meetings laws. BOH compliance with those laws is further discussed in Chapter 12.

During the Adjudication Hearing

During the hearing, the BOH may receive evidence, including oral testimony, from the aggrieved party and other experts or witnesses. The BOH should consult with legal counsel in advance of the hearing to discuss any best practices, due process requirements, or other legal standards related to the presentation of evidence during the hearing. Once the BOH has heard all evidence in the case, it may vote on whether to affirm, modify, or reverse the challenged action.[12]

After the Adjudication Hearing

The BOH's decision to affirm, modify, or reverse the challenged action must be memorialized in a written decision issued by the BOH. The decision must be based on the evidence presented at the hearing and include a brief statement of the reasons for the BOH's determination.[13] The statute does not specify how quickly the BOH must issue its written decision; however, prompt action is recommended, as the BOH's decision is arguably not final until the written decision is issued (and the aggrieved person's timeline for appealing to district court does not begin to run until then).[14]

Once the BOH has rendered its decision, the aggrieved person has a right to further appeal the matter to a district court with jurisdiction. The aggrieved person must file that appeal within thirty days of the BOH's decision. The district court's scope and standard of review for hearing the appeal is set forth in the North Carolina Administrative Procedure Act at G.S. 150B-51(c).[15]

Notes

1. Chapter 130A, Section 24(b) of the North Carolina General Statutes (hereinafter G.S.). Note that although this statute describes appeals "concerning the enforcement of rules adopted by the local board of health *and* concerning the imposition of administrative penalties by a local health director" (emphasis added), the North Carolina Court of Appeals has determined that the word *or* may be substituted for *and* in this provision. *See Justice for Animals v. Robeson County*, 164 N.C. App. 366 (2004) (quoted as saying: "Our review of the grammatical structure of the statutory provision [G.S. 130A-24(b)] reveals that the General Assembly must have intended to allow an appeal either to challenge the enforcement of rules or to challenge the imposition of administrative penalties. Plaintiffs' construction would render the portion relating to 'the enforcement of rules' meaningless since the imposition of administrative penalties will always involve the enforcement of rules").
2. The current rules governing accreditation for local health departments (LHDs) require the BOH to "assure a fair and equitable adjudication process" by following the procedure set out in G.S. 130A-24(b) to (d). These rules are found at Title 10A, Chapter 48B, Section .0102 of the North Carolina Administrative Code. The rules do not specify how the BOH must make this assurance, but some BOHs appear to have done this by adopting policies that reiterate a commitment to complying with the statutorily required process for adjudications. *See, e.g.* Stokes Cnty. Health Dep't Meeting Minutes, July 15, 2019, at 11, https://cms9files.revize.com/stokescountync/administration/Minutes/2019/m071519_doh.pdf#page=11; Halifax Cnty. Bd. of Health Meeting Minutes, January 24, 2022, at 4, https://www.halifaxnc.com/DocumentCenter/View/2944/BOH-Minutes-Jan-24-2022-?bidId=#page=4.
3. G.S. 130A-24(b). There are only two instances where a local health director may impose an administrative penalty: violation of public health smoking laws (state or local) or violation of the on-site-wastewater rules imposed by the BOH (but not the Commission for Public Health). *See* G.S. 130A-22(h) to (h1).
4. G.S. 130A-24(a) to (a1).
5. *In re* Assessment of Additional Sales and Use Taxes Against Halifax Paper Co., 259 N.C. 589, 595 (1963) (quoting 3 C.J.S. *Aggrieved* (n.d.)); *see also* Justice for Animals v. Robeson County, 164 N.C. App. 366 (2004), N.C. Forestry Ass'n v. N.C. Dep't of Env't & Nat. Res., 357 N.C. 640, 644 (2003).
6. G.S. 130A-24(b).
7. Presnell v. Pell, 298 N.C. 715, 721 (1979).
8. G.S. 130A-24(b).
9. *Id.*
10. G.S. 130A-24(c).
11. G.S. 143-318.9. See G.S. 14-318.10(b) for the definition of *public body* and G.S. 14-318.10(d) for the definition of *official meeting.*
12. G.S. 130A-24(c).
13. *Id.*
14. *See* G.S. 130A-24(d).
15. *Id.*

Chapter 11

Ethical Standards and Legal Prohibitions for Board Members

As used in this book, the term *ethics* refers broadly to standards of behavior that the public expects from people who hold public office.[1] When discussing ethical standards related to board service, it is important to distinguish between conduct that is legally prohibited and conduct that merely falls short of ethical norms.

Some conduct by public officials may violate state or federal laws. That conduct is both *unethical* and *illegal.* Other conduct by members of the local board of health (BOH) may violate ethical norms but not actually violate any laws. In other words, that behavior would be *unethical* but not *illegal.*

BOH members should not engage in unethical behavior, regardless of whether the behavior violates the law. Unethical conduct on the part of BOH members can erode the public's trust in the BOH, as well as trust in government institutions more broadly. For purposes of clarity, this chapter will attempt to distinguish between ethical expectations and legal prohibitions.

Ethical Expectations for Public Officials

Basic Standards of Ethical Behavior

The general public expects all public officials, including BOH members, to act ethically in their public and private lives. Based on basic ethical principles, BOH members should

- devote adequate time and energy to their board responsibilities;
- make fair, impartial decisions;
- act in the public interest and for the public good;

This chapter is authored by Kristi A. Nickodem. She has adapted this chapter from her book *Local Social Services Boards in North Carolina* (UNC School of Government, 2023) and revised it to apply specifically to local boards of health.

- not use their offices to benefit themselves, their family members, or their friends;
- exercise sound judgment and discretion in connection with their official duties; and
- act honestly, courteously, and collaboratively when working together as a board.

Conflicts of Interest

The term *conflict of interest* generally refers to a conflict between an individual's personal, family, business, professional, or financial interests and that individual's role, responsibilities, duties, or actions as a public official.[2] Put another way, a conflict of interest occurs when an individual's private interests interfere (or may interfere) with that individual's independence, decision-making, and judgement as a board member.

BOH members should act in the public interest—and not for their own personal benefit—when serving as public officials. They should take reasonable actions to avoid actual and potential conflicts between their personal interests and public responsibilities. When possible, BOH members should avoid even the *appearance* of acting unethically, inappropriately, or for their own benefit.[3] Avoiding conflicts of interest helps the BOH to maintain the public's trust.

If the conflict between an individual's personal interests and professional responsibilities as a BOH member is significant and unavoidable, it may constitute good cause for requesting the BOH member's resignation. If the BOH member refuses to resign, then the board of county commissioners (BOCC) (for a county BOH or consolidated human services board) or the BOH itself (for a district BOH) would have statutory grounds to remove the board member if the member's behavior violated a state law governing conflicts of interest or constituted conduct that tends to bring the board member's office "into disrepute."[4] More information about removal of board members can be found in Chapter 5.

In some cases, making or administering certain contracts (or attempting to influence someone who does) when a board member has a conflict of interest is not only unethical but also illegal. The laws related to conflicts of interest in contracting will be discussed later in this chapter.

Political Activities

BOH members should not use their positions on the board to promote political candidates, parties, or platforms. The BOH should be seen by the public as a nonpartisan, politically neutral entity. When BOH members use their positions on the board to promote political parties or candidates, it can cause members of the public to lose trust in the board's motives and impartiality.

Legally Prohibited Conduct

Involvement with Contracts for Personal Benefit

Chapter 14, Section 234 of the North Carolina General Statutes (hereinafter G.S.) addresses conflicts of interest related to contracts. Specifically, this law prohibits public officials, including BOH members, from the following actions:

- *Prohibition 1:* A board member is prohibited from receiving a direct benefit from a public contract if the board member is involved in *making or administering* the contract.[5]
- *Prohibition 2:* A board member is prohibited from *influencing or attempting to influence* any person involved in making or administering a public contract if the board member will derive a direct benefit from the contract.[6]
- *Prohibition 3:* A board member is prohibited from soliciting or receiving "any gift, favor, reward, service, or promise of reward, including a promise of future employment, in exchange for *recommending, influencing, or attempting to influence* the award of a contract" by the county.[7]

Violating any one of these conflict-of-interest provisions in G.S. 14-234 is a criminal offense (a Class 1 misdemeanor).[8] Moreover, contracts made in violation of the statute are void.[9]

What Is a "Direct Benefit"?

A board member directly benefits from a public contract if the board member or the board member's spouse "(i) has more than a ten percent (10%) ownership or other interest in an entity that is a party to the contract; (ii) derives any income or commission directly from the contract; or (iii) acquires property under the contract."[10]

This means that Prohibitions 1 and 2 relate not only to contracts that may benefit the board member, but also to contracts that may benefit the board member's spouse.

What Does It Mean to "Make or Administer" a Contract?

A public official who "participates in the development of specifications or terms or in the preparation or award of the contract" or who is a member of a board that takes action with respect to the contract (regardless of whether the official participates in the action) is involved in *making* a contract.[11] A public official who "oversees the performance of [a] contract or has authority to make decisions regarding the contract or to interpret the contract" is involved in *administering* a contract.[12]

While district boards of health have legal authority to enter certain types of contracts, appointed county boards of health and consolidated human services (CHS) boards generally lack legal authority to make or administer contracts involving the local health department (LHD).[13] As a result, Prohibition 1 (described earlier) will rarely apply to members of appointed county boards of health or CHS boards. It would be easier for members of those types of boards to run afoul of Prohibition 2 or 3, which involve improperly influencing someone else (such as the local health director or a county commissioner)[14] who is involved in making or administering a contract.

Are There Any Exceptions to These Prohibitions Around Contracts?

There are several exceptions to Prohibition 1, the prohibition against a board member's deriving a direct benefit from a contract that the board member is involved in making or administering.[15]

For example, Prohibition 1 does not apply to an employment relationship between the LHD and the spouse of a BOH member if the BOH member

1. does not participate in deliberating or voting with respect to the making or administering of the contract, and
2. does not attempt to influence any other person (such as the local health director) who is involved in making or administering the contract.[16]

Prohibition 1 also does not apply to a contract involving payment to a BOH member or the member's spouse for services, facilities, or supplies furnished directly to "needy" individuals by the LHD under any federal or state public assistance program if

1. the program is open generally to all providers of services on a nondiscriminatory basis;
2. neither the LHD nor its agents or employees have any control over the selection of participating providers by beneficiaries of the program;
3. the payment for services, facilities, or supplies is in the same amount as would be paid to any other participating provider;
4. the board member does not participate in approving the payment;
5. the board member does not deliberate or vote on the contract; and
6. the board member does not attempt to influence any other person who is involved in making or administering the contract.[17]

There is also a "small jurisdiction" exception to Prohibition 1 for contracts benefitting certain individuals on the BOH. This exception applies to a board member who is a physician, pharmacist, dentist, optometrist, veterinarian, or nurse serving on a BOH in a county where there is no village, town, or city with a population of more than 20,000 people.[18] If a contract provides a direct benefit to a board member who fits that description, the board may still make or administer the contract so long as

1. the contract (or series of contracts) "is approved by specific resolution of the governing body adopted in an open and public meeting, and recorded in its minutes";

2. the amount of the contract "does not exceed twenty thousand dollars ($20,000) for medically related services and sixty thousand dollars ($60,000) for other goods or services within a 12-month period";
3. the board member entering into the contract does not participate in any way or vote;
4. the total annual amount of contracts with the board member is "specifically noted in the audited annual financial statement of the village, town, city, or county"; and
5. the BOH posts "in a conspicuous place in its village, town, or city hall, or courthouse" (e.g., the door of its regular meeting room), "a list of all such officials with whom such contracts have been made" that briefly describes the subject matter of the contracts and shows their total amounts (covering the preceding twelve months and updated at least quarterly).[19]

This exception recognizes the reality that in some less populated counties, a professional serving on the BOH may be the only person available (or one of few) in the county to provide certain necessary services.

Key Takeaways

Learning about the prohibitions in G.S. 14-234 and the exceptions to those prohibitions can feel confusing. Here are some key takeaways to remember:

- Board members should not attempt to influence the local health director or any other public official or employee involved in making or administering a contract if the board member or board member's spouse will receive a direct benefit from the contract.
- Board members should not attempt to influence the local health director or any other public official or employee involved in making or administering a contract in exchange for any gift, favor, reward, service, or promise of reward (regardless of whether the board member receives any direct benefit under the contract).
- If a board member is involved in any way in making decisions about a contract or overseeing the performance of a contract, and the board member knows that the contract may provide a benefit to the board member or the board member's spouse, then the board member should take a step back and consult with the county attorney or other legal counsel prior to taking any action with respect to the contract. The county attorney or other legal counsel will be able to help determine whether the board member's involvement with the contract is permitted under one of the exceptions in the law.

Accepting Gifts and Favors

Another North Carolina statute, G.S. 133-32, makes it a Class 1 misdemeanor for certain public officials and government employees to willfully receive or accept a gift or favor from a contractor, subcontractor, or supplier who has a contract with a governmental agency, has performed under such a contract within the past year, or anticipates bidding on one in the future.[20] Specifically, this prohibition on receiving or accepting gifts or favors applies to any BOH member, local health director, or LHD employee who is involved in (1) preparing plans, specifications, or estimates for public contracts; (2) awarding or administering public contracts; or (3) inspecting or supervising construction.[21]

This statute does not prohibit public officials or government employees from receiving customary gifts or favors from friends and family members, so long as it is clear that the gifts are motivated by preexisting friendships or familial relationships rather than by a desire to do business with a government agency.[22] Likewise, the statute contains exceptions for honorariums, advertising items of nominal value, meals at banquets, donations to professional organizations to defray meeting expenses, and participation in functions at meetings of professional organizations that are available to all attending organization members.[23]

Other Legally Prohibited Conduct

Willful Failure to Discharge Board Member Duties

If a BOH member willfully neglects or refuses to discharge their official BOH duties, the board member can be charged with a Class 1 misdemeanor as a criminal offense.[24] Under some circumstances, the court may remove the board member from public office as part of the sentence for the offense. Habitual failure to attend BOH meetings, which may be one way that a member willfully fails to discharge their duties, is also grounds for removal of the member from the BOH.[25]

Improper Influence Regarding Hiring and Promotion of Department Employees

As described earlier in this chapter, a BOH member is legally prohibited from influencing or attempting to influence the local health director to hire or promote the board member's spouse.[26] It is also unethical for a BOH member to attempt to influence the local health director to hire, promote, or provide preferential treatment to *any* family member or friend of the board member.[27]

State law does not prohibit the local health director from hiring a qualified applicant merely because the person is related to a BOH member. Likewise, an individual is not prohibited from serving on the BOH merely because a spouse or other relative is employed by the LHD. Being related to an LHD employee or applicant for LHD employment does not, by itself, create an ethical conflict for a board member. Rather, ethical conflicts are created when board members use their positions on the board to influence or coerce the local health director to make certain decisions about hiring or promotions.

Board members should also be aware that under State Human Resources Commission rules, the local health director is prohibited from hiring an immediate family member (a spouse, parent, sibling, child, grandparent, or grandchild of the director) to be employed by the LHD.[28]

Improper Use or Disclosure of Confidential Information

State law requires that personnel information for employees of county health departments, district health departments, and consolidated human services agencies be kept confidential, including information regarding job applicants.[29] This means that, except in performance of their board duties, BOH members should not use or disclose information about a local health director's application, selection, performance, promotions, demotions, transfers, suspension, other disciplinary actions, evaluations, leave, compensation, or dismissal.[30] Only certain pieces of information from the director's personnel file are a matter of public record, as listed in G.S. 153A-98(b). A public official (including a BOH member) or employee who knowingly, willfully, and with malice permits any person to have access to personnel-file information in violation of G.S. 153A-98 is guilty of a Class 3 misdemeanor.[31]

Another state law, G.S. 14-234.1, prohibits BOH members from using nonpublic information that they learn through board service for purposes of financially benefiting themselves or others. Specifically, this statute makes it a Class 1 misdemeanor for a board member to acquire a pecuniary interest or gain a pecuniary benefit (or intentionally aid someone else in doing so) if the board member is

1. acting in anticipation of the board member's official action as a board member or action by the LHD, and the pecuniary interest or benefit may be affected by this official action; or
2. relying on nonpublic information that the board member obtained in the member's official capacity, and the pecuniary interest or benefit may be affected by that nonpublic information.

Holding Too Many Public Offices

Under North Carolina law, an individual is prohibited from holding more than

- two appointive public offices at the same time or
- one elective public office and one appointive public office at the same time.[32]

Serving on an appointed BOH is an appointive office; however, a county commissioner appointed to a BOH by the BOCC (an *ex officio* appointment) is deemed to be only holding one elective public office (the office of county commissioner)—not one elected and one appointive public office.[33] In other words, service on a BOH does not count toward the office-holding limit for that commissioner.

Holding Incompatible Offices

In addition to the prohibition on multiple office-holding described above, there is older North Carolina case law recognizing a common law doctrine that prohibits incompatible office-holding.[34] Under this doctrine, two offices are generally "incompatible" when there is a conflict between the functions or duties of the two offices.[35] For example, this would prohibit an individual from holding two offices where one of the offices acts as a supervisor for another (i.e., a superior/subordinate relationship).

For county and district boards, this means that a board member should never serve as acting or interim local health director, since the board has authority to make decisions about the local health director's employment (including evaluating, disciplining, and dismissing the director). Likewise, for CHS boards, this means that a board member should never serve as acting or interim director of the consolidated human services agency, since the board is required to provide advice and consent to the county manager's appointment and dismissal of the director.[36]

Improper Conduct of Board Members Who Are Lawyers

BOH members who are licensed to practice law in North Carolina must comply with the Rules of Professional Conduct (Rules) adopted by the North Carolina State Bar.[37] The Rules prohibit a lawyer who has been appointed to a BOH from considering any matter, participating in any decision, or attempting to influence any issue as a board member in which the lawyer or the lawyer's firm has any direct or indirect interest.[38]

The Rules do not prohibit a lawyer from serving on the BOH merely because the lawyer's partner, associate, or firm represents the BOH or the LHD, so long as the lawyer who serves on the board refrains from participating in any deliberations or actions related to the firm's legal representation of the board or LHD and does not attempt to influence the board's, department's, or county's actions with respect to the firm.[39]

The Rules also prohibit an attorney who serves on the BOH from directly participating in a lawsuit or other matter in which the attorney's firm is adverse to the LHD, the BOH, or the local health director. The attorney's law firm must screen the attorney out from participating in the matter, the BOH must screen the attorney out from participating in the board's discussions or voting on the matter, and the attorney must make certain disclosures to the board about the attorney's relationship to the matter. The attorney board member must also refrain from any expression of opinion, public or private, or any formal or informal consideration of the matter, including any communication with other board members or the local health director about the matter. The attorney's *law firm* is not prohibited from representing a client in such a matter, so long as these requirements are met. However, if the attorney board member is a necessary *party* to the litigation or other adverse action (in either an individual or official capacity), the attorney's firm or partner is disqualified from representing *any* party in the action.[40]

Certain Ethics Laws Applicable to the Local Health Director

Remember, BOH members are public officials, not government employees. This means that they are not subject to some of the ethics laws that may apply to LHD employees, such as the Hatch Act (Title 5 of the U.S. Code, Chapter 15) and G.S. 153A-99 (which applies to county employees). However, board members should be familiar with these ethics laws, since the Hatch Act likely applies to all local health directors and G.S. 153A-99 applies to directors within a county health department or consolidated human services agency.

The Hatch Act[41] is a federal law that prohibits a state or local government employee from running for partisan political office if the employee works in a position that has duties in connection with programs financed in whole or in part by federal funds.[42] G.S. 153A-99 prohibits county employees from (1) using their official authority or influence for the purpose of interfering with or affecting the result of an election or nomination for political office; or (2) coercing, soliciting, or compelling contributions for political or partisan purposes by another employee while on duty or in the workplace. This law also prohibits county employees from requiring other county employees to contribute funds for political or partisan purposes.

Other Laws Applicable to County Commissioners

When the BOCC serves directly as the BOH, the commissioners may be subject to additional ethics and conflict-of-interest requirements (that would not normally apply to appointed boards of health) due to their roles as commissioners. For example, G.S. 153A-44 imposes a duty upon each county commissioner to vote on any matter before the BOCC unless the matter involves certain actual (not merely apparent) conflicts of interest for the commissioner as defined by statute. Appointed BOH members do not have a similar statutory "duty to vote."

A BOCC exercising the powers and duties of a BOH also should be mindful of G.S. 14-234.3, which prohibits a county commissioner who serves as a director, officer, or governing-board member of a nonprofit organization from participating in making or administering any contracts between that nonprofit and the county.[43] Specifically, commissioners who are directors, officers, or governing-board members of a nonprofit must recuse themselves from any deliberation or vote by the BOCC on a contract (including an award of money) with that nonprofit, and the recusal must be recorded with the board's clerk.[44] A knowing violation of G.S. 14-234.3 is a Class 1 misdemeanor.[45]

For more information on compliance with G.S. 14-234.3, please see *Conflicts of Interest for Public Officials on Nonprofit Boards: An Analysis of North Carolina G.S. 14-234.3*, by Kristina Wilson.[46]

Notes

1. For a more in-depth discussion of ethics for public officials (and other definitions of the term *ethics*), please see A. Fleming Bell, II, Ethics, Conflicts, and Offices: A Guide for Local Officials (UNC School of Government, 2d ed. 2011).
2. Conflicts of interest are discussed in more detail in Chapter 4 and Chapter 5 of Bell, *supra* note 1.
3. When the BOCC is acting as the board of health, the county commissioners have a duty to vote unless there is an actual conflict of interest as defined under Chapter 153A, Section 44 of the North Carolina General Statutes (hereinafter G.S.). Members of appointed boards of health do not have a similar statutory duty to vote.
4. G.S. 130A-35(g) (county BOH); G.S. 130A-37(h) (district BOH); G.S. 153A-77(c) (consolidated human services board).
5. G.S. 14-234(a)(1).
6. G.S. 14-234(a)(2).
7. G.S. 14-234(a)(3) (emphasis added).
8. G.S. 14-234(e).
9. G.S. 14-234(f). This statute provides certain exceptions under which the void contract may continue in effect until an alternative can be arranged.
10. G.S. 14-234(a1)(4).
11. G.S. 14-234(a1)(3).
12. G.S. 14-234(a1)(2).
13. Except as otherwise provided by law, the county's authority to enter into contracts must be exercised by the BOCC. G.S. 153A-11. The BOCC could authorize an appointed CHS board or appointed county BOH to approve certain contracts. But if the BOCC has not granted such authority, an appointed CHS board or appointed county BOH has no role or responsibility with respect to the approval of contracts.
14. North Carolina law expressly authorizes a local health director to enter into contracts on behalf of the LHD; however, that grant of power does not abrogate the BOCC's authority. *See* G.S. 130A-41(b)(13).
15. G.S. 14-234(b) lists additional exceptions for other types of contracts that are not described in this chapter.
16. G.S. 14-234(b)(3), (b1).
17. G.S. 14-234(b)(4), (b1).
18. G.S. 14-234(d1). Population size is determined according to the most recent official federal census.
19. G.S. 14-234(d1).
20. G.S. 133-32(a).
21. *Id.*
22. G.S. 133-32(d).
23. *Id.*
24. G.S. 14-230(a).
25. G.S. 130A-35(g) (county BOH); G.S. 130A-37(h) (district BOH); G.S. 153A-77(c) (consolidated human services board).
26. G.S. 14-234(a)(2).
27. If the board member solicits or receives a gift, favor, reward, service, or promise of reward (including a promise of future employment) in exchange for this influence, it may be a violation of G.S. 14-234(a)(3).

28. *See* Title 25, Chapter 01I, Section .1702 of the North Carolina Administrative Code (hereinafter N.C.A.C.). Specifically, the rule states, "Members of an immediate family shall not be employed within the same agency if the employment results in one member supervising another member of the employee's immediate family, or if one member will occupy a position that has influence over another member's employment, promotion, salary administration, or other related management or personnel considerations." In most organizational models, the local health director occupies a position that has influence over the terms and conditions of LHD employees' employment.
29. G.S. 153A-98; *see also* Elkin Trib., Inc. v. Yadkin Cnty. Bd. of Cnty. Comm'rs, 331 N.C. 735 (1992). G.S. 130A-42, which applies to the personnel records of district health departments, makes those records subject to the same statute (G.S. 153A-98) that governs county employee personnel records. G.S. 130A-42 directs the local health director to perform duties assigned to the county manager under G.S. 153A-98 and the district board of health to perform duties assigned to the BOCC under G.S. 153A-98.
30. G.S. 153A-98(a).
31. G.S. 153A-98(e).
32. N.C. Const. art. VI, § 9; G.S. 128-1.1. North Carolina's law limiting multiple office-holding is discussed in detail in A. Fleming Bell, II, *Multiple Office-Holding, in* Ethics, Conflicts, and Offices: A Guide for Local Officials, *supra* note 1, ch. 6.
33. G.S. 128-1.2.
34. For a comprehensive discussion of the common law doctrine of incompatible office-holding, including applicable case law, please see A Fleming Bell, II, *Incompatible Office-Holding, in* Ethics, Conflicts, and Offices: A Guide for Local Officials, *supra* note 1, ch. 7.
35. *See* Bell, *supra* note 1, at 148.
36. G.S. 153A-77(e).
37. The full text of the Rules is available on the North Carolina State Bar's website at https://www.ncbar.gov/for-lawyers/ethics/rules-of-professional-conduct/.
38. N.C. State Bar, Ethics Opinion CPR 290 (Oct. 14, 1981) (overruled in part by N.C. State Bar, Employment of Board Member's Law Firm, Ethics Opinion RPC 130 (Oct. 23, 1992)).
39. N.C. State Bar, Employment of Board Member's Law Firm, *supra* note 38.
40. N.C. State Bar, Implications of Service on a Public Body or Non-Profit Board, 2002 Formal Ethics Op. 2 (July 9, 2002).
41. 5 U.S.C. §§ 1501–08.
42. *See* Diane Juffras, *What Is the Hatch Act?*, UNC Sch. of Gov't, https://www.sog.unc.edu/resources/faqs/what-hatch-act (last visited Apr. 4, 2023).
43. G.S. 14-234.3(a).
44. *Id.* The same exceptions that apply to G.S. 14-234 also apply to this recusal requirement regarding contracts with nonprofits (*see* G.S. 14-234.3(b)), meaning G.S. 14-234.3 does not require a commissioner's recusal from involvement with a contract with a nonprofit if it falls within one of those exceptions. However, the requirements for complying with those exceptions, discussed earlier in this chapter, will generally also mandate the conflicted public official's recusal from involvement with the contract.
45. G.S. 14-234.3(b).
46. Kristina Wilson, *Conflicts of Interest for Public Officials on Nonprofit Boards: An Analysis of North Carolina G.S. 14-234.3,* Loc. Gov't L. Bull. No. 142 (UNC School of Government, Nov. 2022), https://www.sog.unc.edu/sites/default/files/reports/2022-11-21%2020220220%20LGLB%20142.pdf.

Chapter 12
Board Meetings and Procedures

To exercise the board's powers and duties, members of the local board of health (BOH) must act together as a public body in an official meeting.[1] North Carolina's open meetings law (Chapter 143, Article 33C of the General Statutes, hereinafter *G.S.*) establishes multiple requirements for how these meetings must be conducted, which are discussed in this chapter. Outside of the open meetings law, state law also contains requirements for boards of health regarding the frequency of board meetings, the role of the board chair, and the board's voting process. This chapter discusses these legal requirements, along with other procedural matters.

Board Secretary

The local health director serves as the secretary for a county or district BOH.[2] State law allows the local health director to delegate this secretarial duty to another person (e.g., an employee of the local health department).[3] In a county with an appointed consolidated human services (CHS) board, the CHS director (who may or may not also serve as the local health director) acts as secretary to the CHS board.[4] The remainder of this chapter will refer to the local health director as the secretary for the board, but keep in mind that this responsibility lies with the CHS director in a county with an appointed CHS board.

This chapter is authored by Kristi A. Nickodem. She has adapted this chapter from her book *Local Social Services Boards in North Carolina* (UNC School of Government, 2023) and revised it to apply specifically to local boards of health.

Board Meeting Procedures

Frequency of Board Meetings

State law requires each BOH to meet at least quarterly.[5] However, in some cases, the board may need to meet more frequently to accomplish its work. The board chair or any three BOH members may call additional special meetings, if needed.[6]

Date and Time of Board Meetings

Boards may vote to determine the dates and times of their regular board meetings.[7] Most boards establish a consistent day and time for board meetings. Some boards find it more convenient to meet during the workday, while others choose to meet in the evenings to accommodate the work schedules of board members. When deciding on a schedule for regular meetings, the BOH should attempt to choose a time and day of the week that is mutually convenient for board members and the local health director.

Election and Role of the Board Chair

State law requires each BOH to annually elect one of its members to serve as board chair.[8] This election must not be conducted in closed session.[9] Unless the board's procedures or policies provide otherwise, the board chair should be elected by a majority vote of the board members who are currently serving on the board and are present at the meeting.[10] Although a board chair must be elected each year, nothing in state law prohibits the same BOH member from being reelected for additional consecutive one-year terms as chair.

A BOH may also vote to designate another board member as vice-chair, though the board is not required to do so. The board may authorize this individual to exercise the board chair's powers and duties in the event of the chair's absence, death, resignation, or removal from office.

What are the chair's powers and duties?

- The chair is authorized to call additional special meetings of the board outside of the regular meeting schedule.[11]
- The chair has the implied authority and responsibility to preside at board meetings; to ensure that board meetings are conducted fairly and in accordance with the board's rules of procedure; to recognize members who wish to speak at board meetings; and to rule on motions and questions of procedure at board meetings.[12]

Other responsibilities of the BOH chair vary from board to board and person to person. For example, on some boards the board chair functions as the board's primary spokesperson in the community or acts as a liaison between the BOH and other public bodies. On other boards, the board chair presides over meetings but does not act as an external spokesperson or liaison. BOH members should discuss and agree upon their expectations with respect to the chair's role and responsibilities.

Board Meeting Agendas

Preparing and following an agenda for each BOH meeting can help the board be efficient and effective.

The BOH has discretion to develop its own procedures and practices regarding the preparation and circulation of agendas. Generally, the board chair will prepare a proposed agenda for each board meeting with input from the local health director and other board members. The board's secretary will typically send a copy of the agenda and any additional information related to agenda items to board members at least several days before the meeting. As its first order of business at the meeting, the board typically decides whether items should be added to or removed from the proposed agenda, makes any additional changes to the proposed agenda, and adopts the agenda for the meeting.[13]

A BOH should ensure that adequate time is allotted for every item on the meeting agenda. The board's rules of procedure should address the length of board meetings and what the board will do if there is insufficient time to consider all the items on its agenda.

Under state law, the board must provide a copy of the meeting agenda to meeting attendees if the board discusses or acts on matters by reference to a number, letter, or other designation of the matter on the board's agenda and attendees would need a copy of the agenda to understand what the board is referring to.[14]

The agendas for BOH meetings (and all records submitted to the board in connection with BOH meetings) are public records, meaning they must be made available to members of the public upon request except to the extent that they contain information that is confidential or privileged under state or federal laws. Disclosure of public records is discussed in Chapter 13 of this book.

Quorum

A *quorum* is the minimum number of board members that must be present before the board can take any official action or transact public business. If board members act at a meeting at which a quorum is not present, their actions are invalid unless they are subsequently ratified by majority vote of the board at a meeting at which a quorum is present. State law specifies that a majority of BOH members (without regard to vacancies) constitutes a quorum.[15] The local health director is not a member of the board, so the director does not count when determining whether a quorum is present.

Voting

Except as otherwise provided by state law or by a board's rules of procedure, all decisions by a BOH should be made by majority vote of the members who are present and constitute a quorum at an official board meeting. A board member who presides at a meeting as the board's chair or vice-chair retains the right to vote with respect to all issues coming before the board.[16] The local health director may not vote on any matter before the board, since the local health director is not a board member.

The state's open meetings law prohibits BOH members from voting by secret ballot.[17] Board members are allowed to vote by written ballot only if each ballot is signed by the member who voted with it and the minutes of the meeting show how each member voted.[18] The written ballots also must be retained and made available for public inspection in the office of the board's secretary until the minutes of that meeting are approved.[19]

For more information on conflicts of interest that might require board members to recuse themselves from voting, please see Chapter 11 of this book.

Rules of Procedure

Aside from the open meetings law, state law provides little guidance as to procedures for BOH meetings. Accordingly, boards have discretion to establish their own local rules of procedure, so long as those rules do not contradict requirements established by state or federal law. At a minimum, each BOH should consider adopting rules of procedure regarding

- scheduling board meetings;
- determining and circulating the agendas for board meetings;
- conducting business at board meetings;
- electing the board chair;
- remote participation in meetings;
- evaluating the board's work; and
- evaluating the local health director's performance.

The UNC School of Government has developed model rules of procedure for local appointed boards that they can use as a starting point for adopting their own rules of procedure. For more information, please read *Suggested Procedural Rules for Local Appointed Boards*, by Trey Allen and A. Fleming Bell.[20] These suggested rules incorporate the requirements of the state's open meetings law and include model rules regarding board meetings, adoption of meeting agendas, order of business, the duties of the board chair, quorum, minutes, public hearings, appointments, committees, motions, debate, and voting.

Complying with the Open Meetings Law

A BOH is a "public body" for purposes of North Carolina's open meetings law.[21] North Carolina's open meetings law focuses on two main requirements that promote transparency about the meetings of public bodies. First, the public must have *notice* of official meetings of public bodies, and second, the public must have *access* to such meetings. Additionally, the open meetings law requires each public body to keep full and accurate minutes of its official meetings. These requirements, described in more detail in the remaining sections of this chapter, are intended to ensure that members of the public are better informed about how public bodies are carrying out their official responsibilities. As a helpful reference for questions about the open meetings law's requirements, please read *Open Meetings and Local Governments in North Carolina: Some Questions and Answers*, by Frayda Bluestein and David Lawrence.[22]

The open meetings law's requirements regarding public notice and public access are triggered whenever a majority of the board's members meet, assemble, or gather together—in person or via simultaneous electronic or telephonic communication—for the purpose of conducting a hearing, participating in deliberations, voting, or otherwise transacting "public business."[23] This means that board members must be careful to discuss and deliberate on matters of public business related to their board duties only in the context of an official meeting that meets the notice and access requirements of the open meetings law. Even group telephone calls, web conferences, and simultaneous online chat or email threads involving the majority of the board's members have the potential to trigger the requirements of the open meetings law.[24]

Board members can still engage in social gatherings without providing public notice or access, so long as they are not engaging in public business during the gathering and the gathering is not called or held to evade the spirit and purposes of the open meetings law.[25] For example, six members from an eleven-person county BOH could have a dinner party together without triggering the open meetings law's requirements but might violate the open meetings law if they use that dinner party as an opportunity to discuss the setting of fees for environmental health services offered by the local health department (LHD).

Public Notice of Board Meetings

North Carolina's open meetings law requires a BOH to give public notice of all of its official meetings (including those at which all of the board's business will be conducted in closed session) as well as the official meetings of committees or subcommittees of the board.[26] This means that the board may never hold a secret meeting (one without advance notice to the public), even when the entire meeting will be conducted in closed session. The type of public notice that must be given depends on whether the meeting is a regular meeting, a special meeting, an emergency meeting, or a recessed meeting. Table 12.1 defines each type of meeting.

Notice of Regular Meetings

If a BOH establishes a regular date, time, and place for its meetings, the board must file a regular meeting schedule with the clerk for the board of county commissioners (BOCC).[27] For district boards, this meeting schedule should be filed with the board's secretary (the local health director or director's designee).[28] The BOH must also post its regular meeting schedule on either the county's website or the LHD

Table 12.1. Types of Board Meetings

Regular meeting	A meeting held on a regular date and at a regular time and place specified in a schedule filed with the clerk of the board of county commissioners.
Special meeting	Any meeting (other than an emergency or recessed meeting) that is held at a date, time, or place other than the regular date, time, or place specified in the schedule of regular board meetings on file with the clerk.
Emergency meeting	A meeting called because of generally unexpected circumstances that require immediate consideration by the board. Only business connected with the emergency may be considered at an emergency meeting.
Recessed meeting	A continuation (reconvening) of an earlier regular, special, or emergency meeting.

Source: Reprinted from Kristi A. Nickodem, Local Social Services Boards in North Carolina (UNC School of Government, 2023), 130.
Note: See G.S. 143-318.12.

website.[29] Once the board's regular meeting schedule is filed with the appropriate individual and posted online, the BOH does not have to give any additional public notice of any board meeting held at the regular date, time, and location established in the schedule.

If the board wants to change its regular meeting date, time, or location, the secretary or the board chair for a county BOH must file the board's revised regular meeting schedule with the clerk for the BOCC at least seven calendar days before the next regular board meeting that will be held under the revised schedule.[30] For district boards, the revised meeting schedule should be filed with the district board's secretary.[31] The revised schedule must also be posted on either the county's or the LHD's website.[32]

Notice of Special Meetings

Whenever a BOH holds a special meeting, the board must provide notice at least forty-eight hours before the time of the meeting, notifying the public of the date, time, place, and *purpose* of the meeting by

1. posting the notice on the principal bulletin board of the LHD or at the door of the board's usual meeting room;[33]
2. mailing, emailing, or delivering the notice to each person, newspaper, wire service, radio station, and television station that has filed a written request for such notices with the clerk or secretary of the board (often called a "sunshine list");[34] and
3. posting the notice on either the county's or the LHD's website.[35]

If the LHD or the building containing the usual meeting room is closed to the public continuously for forty-eight hours before the time of the special meeting, the notice that is normally posted on the bulletin board or meeting room door must instead be posted on the door of the building (or on the building in an area accessible to the public).[36] If the BOCC is acting as the BOH, the commissioners can only discuss subjects in the special meeting that were listed on the notice of the meeting.[37]

Notice of Emergency Meetings

The board must give public notice of an emergency meeting immediately after board members have been notified of the meeting.[38] The notice must be given to any local newspaper, wire service, radio station, or television station that has filed a written request for such notices with the BOCC clerk or the BOH secretary. The board may give notice of an emergency meeting by email, by telephone, or by the same method used to notify the BOH members of the meeting.

Notice of Recessed Meetings

To continue a meeting at a later time or date, a motion to recess the meeting must be approved by a majority vote of the board. The time and place at which the regular, special, or emergency meeting is to be continued (reconvened) must be announced in open session during the meeting.[39] The time and place of the recessed meeting should also be posted on either the county's or the LHD's website.[40]

Public Access to Board Meetings

Boards may choose the location of their regular BOH meetings. However, the board must consider public accessibility when choosing a location, because the open meetings law requires a public body to take reasonable measures to provide for public access to its official meetings.[41] Among other things, this means the BOH should take reasonable measures to ensure adequate seating for the number of people that typically attend the board's meetings (though the board does not have to provide overflow seating or ensure space for a larger-than-usual crowd).[42] For example, holding a board meeting in a room that is only large enough to provide seating for the board's members may violate the open meetings law if larger rooms are readily available, since using the smaller room would completely exclude members of the public from attending.[43]

The board should also attempt to choose a meeting location that is reasonably accessible to individuals with disabilities and to individuals who must rely on public transportation.[44]

If the BOCC is acting as the BOH, it is generally required to hold all its meetings within the county except in certain circumstances set forth in G.S. 153A-40(c).

Public Comment and Recording at Board Meetings

The open meetings law gives any person the right to attend open sessions of official meetings of a BOH.[45] However, the open meetings law does not give members of the public a right to address the BOH during the board meeting or participate in the board's discussions. A BOH may choose to include a public comment period in its meetings but is not required by law to do so (unless a BOCC is acting as the BOH, in which case the BOCC must provide at least one period for public comment per month at a regular meeting of the board).[46]

The board chair may direct any person, including a board member, to leave a board meeting if the person is willfully interrupting, disrupting, or disturbing the meeting.[47] Willfully refusing to leave the meeting after such an order to leave is given constitutes a Class 2 misdemeanor.[48]

The open meetings law allows any person to photograph, film, tape-record, or otherwise reproduce any part of an open meeting of the BOH.[49] Any radio or television station may also broadcast all or part of an open board meeting. The board may regulate the placement and use of recording or broadcasting equipment if necessary to prevent undue interference with its meetings.[50]

Closed Sessions in Board Meetings

Every official meeting of the BOH must be open to the public.[51] However, sometimes the board needs to hold part of the meeting in "closed session," meaning members of the public are excluded when the board is discussing certain matters. Closed sessions must occur within the context of an official meeting—a meeting that the public has received notice of in accordance with the open meetings law.[52] This means that the BOH cannot hold a secret meeting (one without notice to the public) even if the board intends to conduct all of its business in closed session.

When a BOH holds a closed session, only the board's members have a right to attend. The board may allow the local health director, LHD staff, or others to attend a closed session if the board chooses to do so and their participation will be helpful to the board. However, the board should have a logical justification for who it permits to join a closed session instead of making arbitrary decisions about which members of the public (non-board members) are allowed to attend.[53]

Procedure for Going into Closed Session

Even if most or all of the board's business will be conducted in a closed session, the BOH must start the meeting in open session. To go into closed session, a board member must make a motion (in open session) to go into closed session, and that motion must be adopted by a majority of the board members present and voting.[54]

The motion must state the purpose of the closed session, which must be one (or more) of the permissible purposes listed in G.S. 143-318.11(a).[55] If the purpose is to prevent the disclosure of privileged or confidential information, the motion must state the name or citation of the law that makes the information privileged or confidential. If the purpose is to consult with an attorney and preserve attorney-client privilege, the motion must identify the parties in each existing lawsuit about which the board expects to receive advice during the closed session.

During a closed session, the BOH may not discuss or take action on any matter outside of the purpose(s) specified in the motion to meet in closed session (or outside of the permitted purposes described in G.S. 143-318.11(a)). If the board wants to discuss a different matter in closed session, other than what was specified in the motion, it must reconvene in open session and adopt another motion to meet in closed session for a different permitted purpose.

Permitted Purposes for Closed Sessions

A BOH is not allowed to go into closed session for any reason or to discuss any topic. Instead, the open meetings law provides a limited list of allowable purposes for going into closed session. This means that a BOH may meet in closed session only

- to prevent the disclosure of information that is privileged or confidential under state or federal law or is not considered to be a public record under North Carolina's public records law;[56]
- to consult with an attorney employed or retained by the BOH in order to preserve the attorney-client privilege (but not to discuss general policy matters);[57]
- to consider the qualifications, competence, performance, character, fitness, conditions of appointment, or conditions of initial employment of the local health director (or the director of a consolidated human services agency);[58]
- to hear or investigate a complaint, charge, or grievance by or against the local health director or another LHD employee;[59]
- to plan, conduct, or hear reports concerning investigations of alleged criminal misconduct;[60] or
- to consider or take action with respect to other matters listed in G.S. 143-318.11(a).

Prohibited Purposes for Closed Sessions

The BOH cannot meet in closed session for any purpose other than those listed in the open meetings law at G.S. 143-318.11(a). The open meetings law also explicitly prohibits the board from meeting in closed session for the following purposes.

1. While the board may discuss a *specific* public employee or official (such as the local health director) in closed session, the board may not discuss issues related to general LHD personnel policies in closed session.[61]
2. The board may not take final action to appoint or dismiss the local health director in closed session.[62] However, the board may reach a tentative consensus on such a decision during a closed session and then take the final action to appoint or dismiss the local health director in open session.[63]
3. The board may not use a closed session to consider a board member's qualifications, competence, performance, character, fitness, appointment, or removal, or to discuss or evaluate the board's own performance.[64]

Keeping Minutes of Board Meetings

The open meetings law requires each BOH to keep full and accurate minutes of its official meetings, including closed sessions. Minutes of BOH meetings are typically recorded in written form, but the board may choose to keep minutes in the form of audio or video recordings.[65] The primary purpose of these minutes is to provide evidence that the board's actions followed proper procedure.[66]

The BOH secretary should take minutes of board meetings. If the secretary (the local health director, the CHS director, or their designee) is excluded from a closed session of a board meeting, minutes of the closed session should be taken by a board member (or another person designated by the board who is in the closed session).

For more information about requirements related to keeping minutes, including a more in-depth discussion of some of the topics mentioned in this section, please see *"Full and Accurate" Minutes: A Primer,* by Trey Allen.[67]

Contents of the Minutes

The board's minutes must accurately reflect the substance of all official actions taken by the board and the vote by which action was taken. The board is not required to summarize or quote each member's comments with respect to an issue or to record the names of the members who voted for or against a motion (unless the board voted by written ballot).[68] If the board doesn't take any official action at a meeting, the minutes only need to document that a meeting occurred.[69] However, a board may want to include additional detail in the minutes beyond what is legally required, since the minutes also serve as a historical record of the board's work.[70]

General Accounts of Closed Sessions

If a BOH meets in closed session, the board must (in addition to recording minutes) prepare a "general account of the closed session so that a person not in attendance would have a reasonable understanding of what transpired."[71] The general account of a closed session may consist of a written narrative or an audio or audiovisual recording of the session.

Approving Meeting Minutes

Though not required by the open meetings law, it is important for boards to officially approve the minutes of their meetings. Among other things, this gives board members the opportunity to correct errors in the record. If the board determines that the proposed minutes are incorrect or incomplete, the board may vote to amend the minutes. The motion to approve minutes from a prior meeting should occur in open session, unless the discussion about the minutes or general account of a closed session would "frustrate the purpose" of a closed session held during the previous meeting (for example, by revealing confidential information).[72] In such a case, the board could approve the minutes or general account of the closed session in a subsequent closed session.[73]

Meeting Minutes Are Public Records

The minutes (and proposed minutes) of BOH meetings are public records, meaning they must be made available to a member of the public upon request under the state's public records law except to the extent that they contain information that is privileged or confidential under state or federal law.[74] General accounts and minutes of closed sessions are also public records, but can be withheld from public inspection for "so long as public inspection would frustrate the purpose of a closed session."[75]

The BOH and local health director must preserve the minutes of board meetings—along with meeting agendas and copies of supporting documentation submitted and discussed during meetings—until they are authorized to be destroyed pursuant to a records retention and disposition schedule established by the state Department of Natural and Cultural Resources.[76] The official minutes of board meetings, as well as all attachments necessary to understand the board's actions during a board meeting, must be retained permanently.[77] For more information on records retention and disposition requirements, please see Chapter 13 of this book.

Remote Meetings and Remote Participation

Boards may wish to hold some meetings remotely via teleconference, videoconference, or other electronic means. Under state law, a "remote meeting" is any official meeting with *one or more* members of the public body participating by conference call, conference video, or other electronic means.[78] Before undertaking a remote meeting, a BOH should carefully consider whether such remote participation will jeopardize quorum requirements. Under current North Carolina law, there is clear authority for boards to engage in remote meetings during a declared state of emergency, but the state of the law is less clear with respect to meetings that occur outside a state of emergency. The nuances of this distinction are discussed in more detail below.

Remote Meetings During Emergency Declarations

A special set of requirements apply to remote meetings when the governor or the General Assembly has declared a state of emergency and the board is within the emergency area. Under such circumstances, the board should comply with the requirements of G.S. 166A-19.24, which establishes remote-meeting requirements applicable to public bodies during emergency declarations.[79] This statute provides clear authority for a board to meet remotely during an emergency declaration (assuming the board is in the area covered by the declaration), provided that the board complies with the requirements of G.S. 166A-19.24, including requirements around notice of the meeting, voting, minutes, online streaming, and public hearings. A member of the board participating remotely as allowed under G.S. 166A-19.24 must be counted as present for quorum purposes while simultaneous communication is maintained for that member.[80] Likewise, votes made during a remote meeting under G.S. 166A-19.24 must be counted as if the member were physically present, so long as simultaneous communication is maintained for that member.[81]

Some of the unique requirements of G.S. 166A-19.24 include the following:

- The method of simultaneous communication used by board members participating remotely must allow for any board member to (1) hear what is said by the other board members, (2) hear what is said by any individual addressing the board, and (3) be heard by the other board members when speaking to the board.
- Any board members participating by a method of simultaneous communication in which they cannot be physically seen by the board must identify themselves (1) when the roll is taken or the remote meeting is commenced; (2) prior to participating in the deliberations, including making motions, proposing amendments, and raising points of order; and (3) prior to voting.
- All documents to be considered during the remote meeting must be provided to each member of the board.
- All votes must be conducted by roll call. Voting by secret or written ballots is not permitted.
- The minutes of the remote meeting must reflect that the meeting was conducted by use of simultaneous communication, which members were participating by simultaneous communication, and when such members joined or left the remote meeting.
- All chats, instant messages, texts, or other written communications between board members regarding the transaction of the public business must be treated as public records.[82]
- The remote meeting must be simultaneously streamed live online so that simultaneous live audio (and video, if any) of the meeting is available to the public. If the remote meeting is conducted by conference call, the board must provide the public with an opportunity to dial in or stream the audio live.

Remote Meetings and Participation Outside of a State of Emergency

What about remote meetings held when the governor or the General Assembly has *not* declared a state of emergency, or when the board is outside of the declared emergency area? The current state of the law with respect to whether remote participation counts toward quorum is unclear. In a 2024 case, *State ex rel. Cannon v. Anson County*, the North Carolina Court of Appeals held that only county commissioners who were physically present at a BOCC meeting could be counted toward the quorum "because there was no state of emergency in effect that would have permitted remote participation."[83] However, in March 2025, the North Carolina Supreme Court declared the Court of Appeals' decision in *Anson County* to stand "without precedential value."[84] This means that the *Anson County* decision does not bind future trial courts if the same issues decided in *Anson County* arise in future cases.[85]

The statutes that apply to appointed county boards of health, district boards of health, and CHS boards each state that "[a] majority of the members shall constitute a quorum" (similar to the quorum statute for boards of commissioners), but they do not use the term *present* or indicate that physical presence is required.[86] This statute—combined with the *Anson County* decision that stands without precedential value—leaves uncertainty over whether members participating remotely count toward quorum. In the absence of a binding decision from North Carolina's appellate courts or a change in the law that directly addresses this issue, a cautious approach for boards of health would be to not count remote participants toward quorum for purposes of voting or otherwise conducting board business, unless the board is meeting under a declared state of emergency as authorized by G.S. 166A-19.24.

Ideally, boards of health should address the issue of remote participation in their local rules of procedure, including whether to allow remote participation outside a state of emergency and whether to allow remotely participating members to count toward quorum for voting purposes. Given the complicated legal landscape involved, a board with questions about remote participation by board members should consult with legal counsel.

Special Requirements for Remote Meetings

If the BOH holds a meeting using teleconference or other electronic means, the open meetings law requires the board to provide "a location and means whereby members of the public may listen to the meeting."[87] The board must specify that location information in the notice of the board meeting. At a minimum, this means the board must provide an online meeting link or teleconference information to the public in advance of the meeting.[88]

The open meetings law does not require the board to provide any way for members of the public to speak to or communicate with the board during a remote meeting. In other words, members of the public must be able to *hear* the board meeting, but the board does not have to provide a method for the public to *contribute* to the board meeting. However, a board may want to provide a way for members of the public to speak during remote meetings if the board has decided (in its own rules of procedure) to routinely allow public comment periods during its meetings.

Liability for Violating the Open Meetings Law

Any person who believes that the BOH has violated the open meetings law may seek injunctive relief in district or superior court.[89] If a judge finds that the board violated the open meetings law, the judge may enjoin the board from threatened or continuing violations of the open meetings law or the recurrence of past violations of the law.[90]

Likewise, any individual may file a lawsuit in superior court requesting the entry of a judgment declaring that an action of the BOH was taken, considered, discussed, or deliberated in violation of the open meetings law.[91] If a superior court judge makes such a finding, the judge may declare the action taken by the board in violation of the law to be null and void.[92]

If a court finds that the BOH has violated the open meetings law, the court may order the board to pay the attorney's fees of the person or entity that sued the board. If the court finds that a board member knowingly or intentionally violated the open meetings law, the court may order the board member to *personally* pay all or part of the plaintiff's attorney's fees. However, there is some protection from this potential personal liability: the court may not order a board member to pay the plaintiff's attorney's fees if the board member (or the board as a whole) sought and followed the advice of an attorney with respect to the board's actions.[93] Accordingly, if the board is confused or unclear about the open meetings law's requirements with respect to a certain decision or procedure, the board should consult with an attorney before acting, if possible.

Notes

1. *Public body* is defined at Chapter 143, Section 318.10(b) of the North Carolina General Statutes (hereinafter G.S.). County and district boards of health and consolidated human services boards meet the definition of public body.
2. G.S. 130A-35(e) (county BOH); G.S. 130A-37(f) (district BOH).
3. G.S. 130A-6.
4. G.S. 153A-77(e)(4).
5. G.S. 130A-35(i) (county BOH); G.S. 130A-37(j) (district BOH); G.S. 153A-77(c) (consolidated human services board).
6. G.S. 130A-35(i) (county BOH); G.S. 130A-37(j) (district BOH); G.S. 153A-77(c) (consolidated human services board).
7. If the board chair calls a special or emergency meeting, the chair may determine the date and time of that meeting. However, the chair should attempt (to the extent possible) to choose a reasonable date and time when board members are likely to be available. The same principle applies when three members of the board act together to call a special or emergency meeting.
8. G.S. 130A-35(e) (county BOH); G.S. 130A-37(f) (district BOH); G.S. 153A-77(c) (CHS board).
9. G.S. 143-318.11(a)(6) (prohibiting a public body from considering the qualifications or appointment of a member during a closed session of an official meeting). The fact that a board member has been nominated to serve as chair does not disqualify the nominee from participating in the election of the board's chair.
10. This vote should include newly appointed board members if they have taken their oaths of office.
11. G.S. 130A-35(i) (county BOH); G.S. 130A-37(j) (district BOH); G.S. 153A-77(c) (CHS board).
12. Any board member may make a motion to appeal the chair's decision regarding a procedural matter, and the board may affirm or reverse the chair's decision by majority vote.
13. The agenda may be changed during the meeting after its adoption, but only by a majority vote of the board.
14. G.S. 143-318.13(c).
15. G.S. 130A-35(f) (county BOH); G.S. 130A-37(g) (district BOH); G.S. 153A-77(c) (CHS board).
16. The board chair or vice-chair cannot, however, cast a *second* vote as a tie-breaker.
17. *See* G.S. 143-318.13(b).
18. *See id.*
19. *See id.*
20. Trey Allen & A. Fleming Bell, II, Suggested Procedural Rules for Local Appointed Boards (UNC School of Government, 2020).
21. *See* G.S. 143-318.10(b) (defining *public body*).
22. Frayda S. Bluestein & David M. Lawrence, Open Meetings and Local Governments in North Carolina: Some Questions and Answers (UNC School of Government, 8th ed. 2017).
23. G.S. 143-318.10(d).
24. *But see* NC Citizens for Transparent Gov't, Inc. v. Village of Pinehurst, 910 S.E.2d 288, 292 (N.C. Ct. App. 2024) (finding that when limited email communication takes place hours or days apart, it does not constitute "simultaneous communication" for purposes of the open meetings law).
25. G.S. 143-318.10(d).

26. G.S. 143-318.12.
27. G.S. 143-318.12(a)(2).
28. G.S. 143-318.12(a)(4).
29. *See* G.S. 143-318.12(d). The statute imposes this requirement "if a public body has a Web site." Some counties have a web page where notices of board meetings (including local appointed boards) are typically posted. In other counties, information about the BOH may be customarily posted to a separate website or to a subpage devoted to the county LHD. The clerk to the BOCC may be able to advise a BOH on the best location for this web-based notice.
30. *See* G.S. 143-318.12(a).
31. G.S. 143-318.12(a)(4).
32. *Id.* See *supra* note 29 regarding this requirement.
33. G.S. 143-318.12(b)(2).
34. *Id.* The board may require each newspaper, wire service, radio station, and television station submitting a written request for notice to renew the request annually. The board may require individual persons (other than the media) to renew their requests for notice quarterly.
35. G.S. 143-318.12(e). See *supra* note 29 regarding this requirement. For special meetings, this notice requirement technically only applies if the website is maintained by an employee of the public body. However, best practice is to provide this online notice regardless of who maintains the website, since many members of the public use county websites to stay informed about meetings of their elected and appointed officials.
36. G.S. 143-318.12(b)(2).
37. G.S. 153A-40(b).
38. G.S. 143-318.12(b)(3).
39. G.S. 143-318.12(b)(1).
40. G.S. 143-318.12(e). See *supra* note 29 regarding this requirement. For recessed meetings, this notice requirement technically only applies if the website is maintained by an employee of the public body. However, best practice is to provide this online notice regardless of who maintains the website, since many members of the public use county websites to stay informed about meetings of their elected and appointed officials.
41. G.S. 143, art. 33C; Garlock v. Wake Cnty. Bd. of Educ., 211 N.C. App. 200, 223 (2011).
42. Hildebran Heritage & Dev. Ass'n v. Town of Hildebran, 252 N.C. App. 286, 294 (2017) (finding that a lack of overflow seating or external speakers, absent more, did not constitute an unreasonable failure of access under the open meetings law).
43. *See Garlock*, 211 N.C. App. at 226–27.
44. The open meetings law does not require special accommodations at public meetings for a disabled member of the public, as opposed to a nondisabled member of the public. However, other state and federal statutes that govern access to public facilities by persons with disabilities (such as the Americans with Disabilities Act, 42 U.S.C. § 12101–12213, and the Persons with Disabilities Protection Act, G.S. 168A) may impose such reasonable accommodation requirements.
45. G.S. 143-318.10(a).
46. G.S. 153A-52.1.
47. *See* G.S. 143-318.17.
48. *Id.*
49. G.S. 143-318.14(a).
50. G.S. 143-318.14(b).
51. G.S. 143-318.10(a).
52. G.S. 143-318.11(c).
53. See Question 87 in Bluestein & Lawrence, *supra* note 22.
54. G.S. 143-318.11(c).

55. G.S. 143-318.11(c).
56. G.S. 143-318.11(a)(1). *See also* G.S. 153A-98 (making county employee personnel file information confidential).
57. G.S. 143-318.11(a)(3). The mere fact that an attorney retained or employed by a BOH participates in a board meeting does not in itself justify holding a closed session. To go into closed session, the board must be discussing a legal issue with the attorney that necessitates acting to preserve attorney-client privilege. This could include discussing potential, threatened, or active litigation, but the allowable discussion is not limited to litigation-related matters so long as some legal issue is involved. If the board has approved or considered a settlement in closed session, the terms of that settlement must be reported to the board and entered into its minutes as soon as possible within a reasonable time after the settlement is concluded.
58. G.S. 143-318.11(a)(6).
59. *Id.* A BOH generally has no authority to investigate or hear complaints, charges, or grievances from LHD employees unless they have been made against the local health director. In that instance, the board may find it necessary to investigate or hear such matters in order to determine whether there is a basis for disciplining or dismissing the director.
60. G.S. 143-318.11(a)(7).
61. G.S. 143-318.11(a)(6).
62. *Id.*
63. *See* Maready v. City of Winston-Salem, 342 N.C. 708, 732 (1996).
64. G.S. 143-318.11(a)(6).
65. G.S. 143-318.10(e).
66. See Question 178 in Bluestein & Lawrence, *supra* note 22.
67. Trey Allen, *"Full and Accurate" Minutes: A Primer,* Loc. Gov't L. Bull. No. 140 (UNC School of Government, Jan. 2019), https://www.sog.unc.edu/publications/bulletins/full-and-accurate-minutes-primer.
68. G.S. 143-318.13(b).
69. See Question 178 in Bluestein & Lawrence, *supra* note 22; *see also* Maready v. City of Winston-Salem, 342 N.C. 708, 733 (1996).
70. See Question 178 in Bluestein & Lawrence, *supra* note 22.
71. G.S. 143-318.10(e).
72. *See id.*
73. For more information about the topic of approving confidential closed-session minutes (including other options for doing so), please see Frayda Bluestein, *How to Approve Minutes and General Accounts of Closed Sessions,* Coates' Canons: NC Loc. Gov't L. (June 5, 2018), https://canons.sog.unc.edu/2018/06/how-to-approve-minutes-and-general-accounts-of-closed-sessions/.
74. G.S. 143-318.10(e).
75. *Id.*
76. *See* N.C. Dep't of Nat. & Cultural Res., General Records Schedule: Local Government Agencies, items 1.47, 1.54 (Oct. 1, 2021), https://archives.ncdcr.gov/government/local (scroll to the table and select General Records Schedule: Local Government Agencies).
77. *See id.*, item 1.54.
78. G.S. 166A-19.24(i).
79. If the board's own rules of procedure conflict with the requirements in G.S. 166A-19.24, the board should follow G.S. 166A-19.24.
80. G.S. 166A-19.24(c).
81. G.S. 166A-19.24(d).

82. Like other records created by the board, these electronic communications may be withheld from the public if they were created during a closed session and disclosing them to the public would "frustrate the purpose" of the closed session. *See* G.S. 143-318.10.
83. State *ex rel.* Cannon v. Anson County, 295 N.C. App. 152, 163 (2024), *aff'd, ordered not precedential*, 912 S.E.2d 379 (N.C. 2025).
84. State *ex rel.* Cannon v. Anson County, 912 S.E.2d 379 (N.C. 2025). The North Carolina Supreme Court denied the plaintiff-appellant's petition for discretionary review, leaving the decision of the Court of Appeals "undisturbed but without precedential value." Accordingly, it is unclear why the Supreme Court decided to order the Court of Appeals decision without precedential value. For a discussion of the procedural issues involved, see the concurring and dissenting opinions in *Mole' v. City of Durham*, 384 N.C. 78, 79 (2023).
85. *See generally* John V. Orth, *"Without Precedential Value"—When the Justices of the Supreme Court of North Carolina Are Equally Divided*, 93 N.C. L. Rev. 1719 (2015).
86. G.S. 130A-35(f) (county boards of health); G.S. 130A-37(g) (district boards of health); G.S. 153A-77(c) (CHS boards); *see also* G.S. 153A-43 (defining quorum for a BOCC as "[a] majority of the membership of the board of commissioners.").
87. G.S. 143-318.13.
88. In light of modern technological advances, it is unclear whether the requirement to "provide a location and means whereby members of the public may listen to the meeting" is satisfied by simply providing an online link or teleconference-access information, or whether a public body is still required to provide a physical space and equipment for the public to listen to the remote meeting. A cautious approach would be to provide access to a room in a county building with a telephone, computer, or projector where members of the public could listen to the meeting.
89. G.S. 143-318.16; G.S. 143-318.16A.
90. G.S. 143-318.16(a).
91. G.S. 143-318.16A.
92. G.S. 143-318.16A(a).
93. G.S. 143-318.16B.

Chapter 13
The Public Records Law

Members of the general public have a right to inspect or copy any record that a member of the board of health (BOH), local health director, or employee of a local health department (LHD) makes or receives "in the transaction of public business."[1] This broad right of access is established by North Carolina's public records laws, in Chapter 132 of the North Carolina General Statutes (hereinafter G.S.). The scope of the public's right of access to records, limitations on public access to records, and records retention requirements are all discussed in this chapter.

What Is a Public Record?

Public record refers to any document, paper, letter, map, book, photograph, film, sound recording, tape recording, electronic data-processing record, email, text message, artifact, or other documentary material that is made or received in connection with the transaction of public business by any agency of North Carolina government or its subdivisions (including boards of health and local health departments).[2]

It is the content and purpose of a record—not its location—that determines whether it is subject to the public records law.[3] For example, text messages or emails sent or received by board members on their personal cell phones or through their personal email accounts may be public records if they involve the transaction of public business.

The Right to Access Public Records

Any member of the public has a right to inspect and examine public records "at reasonable times and under reasonable supervision."[4] Likewise, any member of the

---

This chapter is authored by Kristi A. Nickodem. She has adapted this chapter from her book *Local Social Services Boards in North Carolina* (UNC School of Government, 2023) and revised it to apply specifically to local boards of health.

public has the right to obtain copies of public records, which must be furnished "as promptly as possible" following a request for such copies.[5] The public records law does not define "reasonable times" or "as promptly as possible," which leaves some ambiguity about how much time public officials have to respond to records requests. This will depend on factors such as the nature of the request, the availability of personnel to respond to the request, the location of the records, and whether the records must be redacted before being produced.[6]

A public agency or board's obligation to fulfill requests for inspection or copies of public records can be satisfied by making a record available online in a format that allows someone to view the records and to print or save them.[7]

Limitations on the Right to Access Public Records

The right to access public records is not absolute. Many state laws create exceptions to the public's right to access public records, either by making the records confidential or by exempting them from public access.[8] The BOH must not disclose any record in response to a public records request if that record is confidential under state or federal law.

Some of the exceptions to the right of access that are most relevant to boards of health are described below.

Closed-Session Minutes or General Accounts

Meeting minutes and general accounts recorded by the board during a closed session may be withheld from the public "so long as public inspection would frustrate the purpose of a closed session."[9]

Personnel Records

Except in limited circumstances described in G.S. 153A-98, the board may not disclose any personnel file information regarding a current or former LHD director (or any other LHD employee).[10] However, state law (G.S. 153A-98(b)) establishes a list of information about county or district LHD employees that *is* a matter of public record and must be disclosed upon request.[11]

Attorney-Client Communications

The board may withhold from the public any communications by an attorney made within the scope of the attorney-client relationship concerning (1) any claim by or against the BOH, the LHD, or the county, or (2) the prosecution, defense, settlement, or litigation of any judicial action or administrative proceeding to which the board is a party or by which the board may be directly affected.[12] However, these communications become public records three years from the date they are received by the BOH.

Sensitive Identifying Information

The BOH may not disclose information that can be used to access a person's financial resources, such as a person's social security number, tax identification number, driver's license or state identification card number, passport number, checking or savings account number, credit or debit card number, PIN (personal identification number), digital signature, biometric data, fingerprints, or passwords.[13] Exceptions exist in state law for criminal investigation information, trial preparation materials, medical records, contract bid documents, and records involving public security, among others.

What if a requested record contains some information that is confidential and other information that is public record? Unless the law prohibits the disclosure of an *entire* record, the BOH should redact any confidential or nonpublic information and then disclose the public (nonredacted) parts of the record in response to a records request.[14] Whenever possible, the BOH should consult with legal counsel before disclosing any records to ensure that the information being disclosed is not confidential.

Records Versus Information

It is important to remember that the public records law gives the public a right to access existing *records*, not *information*. This means that if a member of the public asks for a record that does not already exist, the BOH is not obligated to compile information or create a *new* record in response to the request.[15]

There is one important exception to this general rule, which relates to personnel information. As described earlier in this chapter, state law makes most personnel file information confidential but also establishes a list of personnel information (not just records) that must be made available upon request. The following information is a matter of public record about any county employee or district LHD employee (including the local health director), and it must be provided upon request even if it is not part of an existing record:

- the employee's name;
- the employee's age;
- the date of the employee's original employment or appointment;
- the terms of any employment contract, whether written or oral;
- the employee's current position, title, and salary;
- the date and amount of each increase or decrease in the employee's salary (including pay, benefits, incentives, bonuses, and deferred and all other forms of compensation);
- the date and type of the employee's most recent promotion, demotion, transfer, suspension, separation, or other change in position classification;
- the date and general description of the reasons for each promotion;

- the date and type of each dismissal, suspension, or demotion for disciplinary reasons (if the disciplinary action was a dismissal, the written notice of the final decision setting forth the basis of the dismissal is also a matter of public record); and
- the office or station to which the employee is currently assigned.[16]

Responsibility for Responding to Public Records Requests

Who is responsible for responding to public records requests on behalf of a BOH? The public records law states that the "custodian of public records" is responsible for responding to such requests and defines the custodian as "[t]he public official in charge of an office having public records."[17] The local health director is the records custodian for all records created or maintained by the LHD. It is less clear who should act as the custodian of records created or maintained by a BOH.[18]

In some counties, the clerk to the BOCC may serve (either by policy or practice) as the custodian of records created by appointed county boards, including a county BOH or consolidated human services board. In a county where this is not the case, or for a district BOH, the BOH could designate its board chair to serve as the board's custodian of records in its rules of procedure. A district BOH could also select the board's secretary (the local health director or the director's designee) as the custodian of records for the BOH.

In any case, each BOH member is a public official and retains responsibility for preserving records that are in the board member's custody. BOH members should work together to respond to public records requests, and they should seek input from the county clerk and legal counsel to determine whether a record can or should be disclosed to the public.

Liability for Denial of Access to Records

Any person who is denied access to public records or copies of public records may seek a court order compelling disclosure or copying of the records.[19] If a party successfully compels the disclosure of public records from the BOH, the court must allow that party to recover its reasonable attorneys' fees from the county (for county or consolidated human services boards) or the district health department (for district boards).[20] However, the court may not assess attorneys' fees if the court finds that the BOH acted in reasonable reliance on

- a court judgment or order applicable to the BOH;
- the published opinion of a North Carolina appellate court, an order of the North Carolina Business Court, or a final order of a North Carolina superior or district court; or
- a written opinion, decision, or letter of the North Carolina Attorney General.[21]

A BOH member may be found *personally* liable for all or part of the attorneys' fees owed to a plaintiff if the court finds that the board member knowingly or intentionally committed, caused, permitted, suborned, or participated in a violation of the public records law. However, a board member cannot be held personally liable for such fees if the member sought and followed the advice of an attorney with respect to the public records request at issue.[22] Because of this potential shield from personal liability, it is prudent for BOH members to consult with an attorney when deciding whether to withhold records in response to a public records request.

Records Retention Requirements

Public officials, including BOH members, are prohibited from destroying, selling, loaning, or disposing of any public record except as allowed by a records retention and disposition schedule established by the North Carolina Department of Natural and Cultural Resources (NC DNCR).[23] These schedules determine how long certain categories of records must be retained and when they may be disposed of or destroyed. The current retention and disposition schedules for local governments are available on the NC DNCR website.[24]

Many of a board's records (such as meeting minutes) fall under categories described in the general records schedule for local government agencies. That schedule must be approved by the BOCC (or, for a district BOH, by the BOCC for each county served by the district health department). The BOH should obtain a copy of the county's approved general records schedule to ensure that BOH members are properly preserving and disposing of records.

The records of an LHD fall under the records retention and disposition schedule for local health departments.[25] The BOH chair and the local health director must sign the schedule to acknowledge that they agree to comply with the LHD retention and disposition schedule requirements.[26] That acknowledgement should be made in a regular BOH meeting and recorded as an action in the board's meeting minutes. A signed copy of the signature page must be sent to the NC DNCR Records Analysis Unit, Government Records Section, 4615 Mail Service Center, Raleigh, NC 27699-4615, or faxed to 919-715-3627. If board members are unsure whether NC DNCR has a signed copy of the schedule for their LHD on file, they may contact a records management analyst at NC DNCR for confirmation.[27]

Notes

1. Chapter 132, Section 1 of the North Carolina General Statutes (hereinafter G.S.).
2. G.S. 132-1(a).
3. *See* Frayda S. Bluestein, Public Records in North Carolina, UNC School of Government (2012), https://www.sog.unc.edu/sites/default/files/course_materials/public_records_overview.pdf (updated and revised from a previous paper authored by David M. Lawrence).
4. G.S. 132-6(a).
5. *Id.*
6. *See* Bluestein, *supra* note 3.
7. G.S. 132-6(a1).
8. Many records that are generated and maintained by the LHD are confidential or are otherwise not public records under North Carolina's public health laws or under federal laws such as HIPAA. BOH members and members of the general public do not have a right of access to such records under North Carolina's public records law (or in some cases, they may only have a right to access a redacted version of a record).
9. G.S. 143-318.10(c).
10. G.S. 153A-98 applies to personnel information for county employees. G.S. 130A-42, which applies to the personnel records of district health department employees, makes those records subject to the same statute (G.S. 153A-98) that governs county employees' personnel records.
11. *See* G.S. 153A-98, 130A-42.
12. G.S. 132-1.1(a).
13. G.S. 132-1.10(b)(5).
14. *See* G.S. 132-6(c).
15. *See* G.S. 132-6.2(e).
16. G.S. 153A-98(b); *see also* G.S. 130A-42 ("[P]ersonnel records of a district health department shall have the same protections from disclosure as county employee personnel records under G.S. 153A-98.").
17. G.S. 132-6(a), -2.
18. For a discussion regarding problems with the records-custodian concept as it is defined in the public records law, see Frayda Bluestein, *Custodians of Public Records,* Coates' Canons: NC Loc. Gov't L. (Dec. 19, 2014), https://canons.sog.unc.edu/2014/12/custodians-of-public-records/.
19. G.S. 132-9(a).
20. G.S. 132-9(c).
21. *Id.*
22. *Id.*
23. G.S. 132-3(a), 121-5.
24. *Local Government Agencies,* State Archives of N.C. (last visited Feb. 21, 2024), https://archives.ncdcr.gov/government/local.
25. In the case of a consolidated human services agency, some of the agency's records might fall under the records retention and disposition schedule for local departments of social services or other local human services agencies that have their own schedules for records retention and disposition.

26. *See* N.C. Dep't of Nat. & Cultural Res., Records Retention and Disposition Schedule: Local Health Departments i–ii (Mar. 1, 2019), https://archives.ncdcr.gov/local-health-departments-schedule/open; *see also* G.S. 121-5(c).
27. *See Directory of Records Management Analysts for Local Government Agencies,* State Archives of N.C. (last visited Jan. 21, 2024), https://archives.ncdcr.gov/government/local/analysts.

Chapter 14
Legal Liability and Immunity

A local health department (LHD) and local board of health (BOH) can be held legally liable and face consequences for their actions (or inactions). While lawsuits against boards of health and their members are relatively rare, the actions of a local health director or LHD employees are a more frequent source of litigation.

This chapter will discuss the ways in which liability can arise from lawsuits related to boards of health and local health departments, the types of immunity available, and the board's role in helping to reduce the risks of such liability.[1]

Lawsuits Against Board Members

An individual may file a civil lawsuit against BOH members in either their official capacities or their individual capacities. Alternatively, an individual may bring legal claims against board members in *both* their official and individual capacities. The difference between *official capacity claims* and *individual capacity claims* is a big one. It determines who is potentially liable for damages in the lawsuit and what types of immunity are available to the named board members.

Official Capacity Claims

A lawsuit against a member of a county BOH or a consolidated human services (CHS) board in the member's official capacity based on the board's alleged violation of state or federal law is, in essence, a lawsuit against the *county itself*.[2] An appointed county BOH, CHS board, or board of county commissioners is not an entity that is legally capable of being sued where the county is the real party in interest.[3]

By contrast, a lawsuit against a district BOH member in the member's official capacity based on the board's alleged violation of state or federal law is a lawsuit against the district BOH itself.[4]

This chapter is authored by Kristi A. Nickodem. She has adapted this chapter from her book *Local Social Services Boards in North Carolina* (UNC School of Government, 2023) and revised it to apply specifically to local boards of health.

In both instances, even though individual board members are named as defendants, an official capacity lawsuit does not seek to hold the individual board members liable. This means that if a monetary judgment is entered against board members in their official capacities, the legal responsibility for paying the judgment lies with the county (for county and CHS boards) or the district BOH, and not with the individual board members. Likewise, if the local health director is sued in the director's official capacity, the lawsuit seeks to recover monetary damages from the county (for a county health department or a consolidated human services agency) or the district health department, not from the director personally.

If an official capacity lawsuit is filed against BOH members, the board and the affected members should immediately contact the board's legal counsel regarding the lawsuit.

Individual Capacity Claims

A lawsuit that names a board member in the member's individual capacity is alleging that the board member is *personally* liable.[5] This means that if a monetary judgment is entered against the board member, the legal responsibility for paying the judgment lies with the individual board member. Likewise, if the local health director is sued in the director's individual capacity, the lawsuit is seeking to hold the director personally liable for a violation of the law.

If a lawsuit names a board member as a defendant in the member's individual capacity, the board member may want to consider seeking advice from independent legal counsel (that is, an attorney other than the attorney for the BOH).

Liability Under the Open Meetings Law and Public Records Law

Please refer to Chapter 12 for information about liability under the open meetings law and Chapter 13 for information about liability under the public records law. If a BOH member knowingly and intentionally violates North Carolina's open meetings law or public records law, a court may order the board member to personally pay all or part of a plaintiff's attorney's fees.[6] However, a board member cannot be held personally liable for such fees under either law if the board member sought and followed the advice of an attorney with respect to the action or records request at issue.[7]

Liability and Immunity for Tort Claims

Sometimes lawsuits involving an LHD or BOH turn on a question of tort liability. A tort is a wrongful act or omission (other than a criminal act or breach of contract) that causes some form of harm or injury and for which courts will provide a remedy (typically in the form of monetary damages).[8]

To succeed in a tort lawsuit, the injured party (the plaintiff) must generally demonstrate that a defendant violated a duty owed to the plaintiff and that the violation caused harm to the plaintiff or the plaintiff's property.[9]

Categories of Torts

There are two primary categories of torts.[10]

Negligence torts involve a failure to exercise the standard of care that a reasonably prudent person would have exercised in a similar situation.[11] A person may only be liable for negligence if that person had a duty to act according to a particular standard of care, failed to do so, and thereby caused harm to another person or property. For example, a local health department or its employees might face a lawsuit based on allegations of negligence in approving a septic system,[12] negligent retention and supervision of a health department employee,[13] or negligent misrepresentation of whether a property was suitable for supporting a septic tank.[14]

Intentional torts, by contrast, are committed by someone acting with intent to engage in a wrongful act.[15] Examples of intentional torts include battery (nonconsensual touching of the body of another with the intent to cause harmful or offensive contact), intentional infliction of emotional distress, and defamation.

Governmental Immunity for Tort Claims

In North Carolina, when a lawsuit is brought against a county (for a county BOH or CHS board) or a district BOH, a legal doctrine known as *governmental immunity* protects the county or district BOH from liability for tort claims so long as (1) the claim arises from the performance of governmental (as opposed to proprietary) functions, and (2) the governmental entity has not waived its immunity through the purchase of liability insurance.[16] Most, if not all, of the activities performed by BOH members are governmental in nature, meaning that a BOH will generally be shielded from liability for tort claims arising from those activities.

Governmental immunity does not apply to BOH members in the rare instances when they are sued in their *individual* capacities. However, as discussed in the following section, a different type of immunity—public official immunity—may apply to those claims.[17]

Public Official Immunity from Tort Claims Against Board Members and Local Health Directors

If a BOH member or local health director is sued in their individual capacity, a legal doctrine known as *public official immunity* may apply. It protects a public official (including a BOH member or local health director) from personal liability for claims alleging negligence in the exercise of the judgment and discretion with which the official is invested by virtue of the office.[18] However, this immunity is not absolute.

Public official immunity does not apply if the board member's or local health director's "act, or failure to act, was corrupt or malicious" or if the board member or local health director "acted outside of and beyond the scope of his duties."[19]

Additionally, some North Carolina Court of Appeals decisions have held that public official immunity applies only to mere negligence claims, meaning that it does not protect board members or local health directors who are sued in their individual capacities for *intentional* torts.[20]

Limitations to Governmental Immunity and Public Official Immunity

It is important to remember that governmental immunity and public official immunity apply only to tort claims. These immunity doctrines do not protect against legal claims alleging

- breach of a valid contract;[21]
- violations of a person's rights under the United States Constitution (see below);
- violations of federal law, such as Title VII of the Civil Rights Act of 1964, the Americans with Disabilities Act, the Age Discrimination in Employment Act, or federal criminal laws; or
- violations of state law, such as the public records law, the open meetings law, state criminal laws, or public health laws found in G.S. 130A.

Liability and Immunity for Claims Under 42 U.S.C. § 1983

Sometimes a lawsuit involving an LHD alleges a violation of an individual's rights under the United States Constitution. In such a case, the claim is typically brought under 42 U.S.C. § 1983 (often called *Section 1983*), a federal statute that authorizes a person to sue and receive injunctive relief or monetary damages from a local government or local government official if the government's conduct or a public official's conduct violates the person's rights under the United States Constitution or certain federal statutes.[22]

The local health director and their employees may be sued for prospective injunctive relief under Section 1983 (typically meaning the lawsuit seeks a court order stopping the agency's officials and employees from engaging in certain conduct in the future). Under certain circumstances, counties may also be held liable for monetary damages in Section 1983 lawsuits that involve the conduct of their officials or employees.[23] Section 1983 lawsuits frequently allege violations of federal constitutional rights, such as the First Amendment right to free speech or the Fourteenth Amendment right of due process.

Section 1983 claims may also be brought against public officials or public employees in their individual capacities. Board members and local health directors, like other public officials, may be held personally liable for monetary damages under Section 1983 when sued in their individual capacities. However, a legal doctrine known as *qualified immunity* frequently protects them from personal liability. Qualified immunity protects public officials and employees from personal liability under Section 1983 so long as their conduct "does not violate clearly established statutory or constitutional rights of which a reasonable person would have known."[24] A right is clearly established when it is "sufficiently clear that every reasonable official would have understood that what he is doing violates that right."[25] This means that qualified immunity generally protects BOH members, local health directors, and LHD employees from personal liability under Section 1983 unless they are "plainly incompetent or . . . knowingly violate the law."[26]

Criminal Liability

BOH members and local health directors are subject to generally applicable federal and state criminal laws as well as to certain criminal laws that specifically govern the conduct of public officials. For example, a BOH member or a local health director may be held criminally liable for

- unlawfully receiving a direct benefit from a contract that involves the LHD;[27]
- receiving a gift, service, favor, or reward in return for attempting to influence the award of a contract by the LHD (see Chapter 11 for a discussion of direct benefits and of favors for influencing awards);[28]
- willfully disrupting an official meeting of the BOH or another public body;[29]
- assaulting other BOH members, the local health director, an LHD employee, or other individuals;[30]
- embezzling or willfully and corruptly misapplying county funds;[31]
- making a false statement under oath in the context of a lawsuit;[32] or
- willfully failing to discharge duties as a public official.[33]

Lawsuits Related to the Local Health Director's Employment

Civil lawsuits regarding the actions or omissions of a BOH may be filed in response to the board's alleged violation of the State Human Resources Act (when applicable) or federal antidiscrimination laws in connection with the board's recruitment, selection, discipline, or dismissal of the local health director. A county or a district BOH may also face a lawsuit based on allegations that the BOH negligently hired or retained the local health director. Actions taken with respect to the local health director's employment, including the hiring process, are the most likely source of potential litigation for the board. Accordingly, the board should be particularly careful to

- document all actions with respect to the local health director's employment, including documenting concerns about the director's

performance or conduct and the steps the board took to address those concerns, and
- seek guidance regarding applicable state and federal employment laws when recruiting, selecting, disciplining, or dismissing the local health director.

Legal Challenges to Local BOH Rules

A BOH or LHD may also encounter legal challenges related to local public health rules promulgated by the board.[34] Every BOH has the authority to adopt rules necessary to protect and promote the public health.[35] BOH rules apply throughout the county or counties served by the BOH and carry the weight of law.[36] For more information about BOH rulemaking, see Chapter 8.

A person who wishes to challenge the enforcement of a BOH rule has thirty days from when the enforcement action at issue was taken to give notice of their appeal to the local health director.[37] Within five working days of receiving such a notice, the local health director must transmit the notice (along with documentation showing the basis for the challenged enforcement action) to the BOH.[38] The BOH must hold a hearing on the appeal and issue a written decision that affirms, modifies, or reverses the challenged action based on evidence presented at the hearing.[39] For more information about this process (known as "adjudication"), see Chapter 10. If the person who challenged the enforcement action is dissatisfied with the outcome of the BOH adjudication, they may contest the BOH's decision through an appeal to district court.[40]

Some legal challenges to BOH rules may arise in the form of declaratory judgment actions filed in superior court, in which a party seeks a declaration from the court that a BOH rule is not legally valid.[41] These cases generally focus on whether the BOH had authority to adopt a certain rule, not how the rule was enforced against a specific party.

Legal Representation and Indemnification of Public Officials

Legal Representation

A county is authorized, but not required, to provide legal representation for a member of a county BOH or CHS board in connection with any civil or criminal action brought against the board member on account of alleged acts or omissions committed in the scope and course of the board member's service on the board.[42] Likewise, a county is authorized, but not required, to provide legal representation for a local health director in connection with any civil or criminal action brought against the director on account of alleged acts or omissions committed in the scope and course of the director's employment.

The county may provide this representation through its own attorney, through a private attorney, or by purchasing insurance that requires the insurer to provide the defense.[43] The board of county commissioners is responsible for deciding whether to provide such legal representation to an individual BOH member or other public official.

State law specifically authorizes (but does not require) district boards of health to contract with their own legal counsel to represent the district BOH members, the district health department, and the district health department's employees.[44] The district BOH is responsible for deciding whether to provide legal representation to an individual BOH member, the district health director, or a health department employee.

Liability Insurance

State law authorizes (but does not require) counties to purchase insurance to protect any of their officers, agents, or employees from civil liability for damages arising from acts or omissions within the scope of their authority and the course of their employment.[45] Likewise, state law authorizes (but does not require) a district BOH to purchase liability insurance for the members of the board and the employees of the district health department.[46]

For counties with a county BOH or a CHS board, the board of county commissioners has discretion to determine what claims and which public officials and employees will be covered by this liability insurance.[47] For a district health department and its BOH, that decision-making authority rests with the BOH itself.[48]

Lawsuits Against the State

In some instances, the actions of LHD employees who work in environmental health may result in liability for the state under the North Carolina State Tort Claims Act.[49] A person who works for an LHD as a registered environmental health specialist (REHS), an REHS intern (REHSI), or a registered environmental health associate (REHA) may be authorized to act on behalf of the state by enforcing certain environmental health rules promulgated by the North Carolina Commission for Public Health (CPH).[50]

REHS, REHSI, and REHA certifications are managed by the State Board of Environmental Health Specialists.[51] Historically, the certified professionals working in this field were referred to as *sanitarians*, and some North Carolina laws and rules continue to use that term today.[52] An REHS or REHSI may be authorized to enforce CPH rules in eight areas: child care and school sanitation; childhood lead-poisoning prevention; food, lodging, and institutions; residential care and migrant housing; on-site wastewater management; public swimming pools; tattoo parlors; and private wells.[53] An REHA reports directly to an REHS and may be authorized to enforce

CPH rules in a subset of the areas in which an REHS works, such as performing inspections of lower-risk (Category I) food establishments.[54]

Although an REHS, REHSI, or REHA is typically an employee or contractor of an LHD, these professionals act as agents of the state when they conduct inspections and enforce environmental health rules adopted by CPH.[55]

In the past, an REHS, REHSI, or REHA working for an LHD was entitled—subject to certain limitations—to legal representation by the North Carolina Office of the Attorney General (AG) for lawsuits related to acts or omissions that occurred in the scope and course of enforcing CPH rules. In 2024, the law governing state and local responsibility for providing legal representation and paying out settlements for lawsuits involving REHS, REHSI, and REHA conduct was amended.[56] As of 2024, each LHD is required to enter into an annual agreement with the North Carolina Department of Health and Human Services (NCDHHS) to provide environmental health services as set forth in G.S. 130A. The agreement must include language regarding quality assurance for all the environmental health services rendered under the agreement. If an LHD enters into the required annual agreement with NCDHHS, then a REHS, REHSI, or REHA who is employed or contracted by the LHD will be defended by the AG in lawsuits brought against them in their official or individual capacities (or both) for acts or omissions made in the scope and course of enforcing CPH rules. However, the state may refuse to defend the REHS, REHSI, or REHA if it determines that

1. the act or omission was not within the scope and course of the REHS, REHSI, or REHA's duties as an authorized agent of the state;
2. the REHS, REHSI, or REHA acted or failed to act because of actual fraud, corruption, or actual malice on their part;
3. defense of the REHS, REHSI, or REHA by the state would create a conflict of interest between them and the state and the REHS, REHSI, or REHA; or
4. defense of the REHS, REHSI, or REHA would not be in the state's best interests.[57]

If the AG does provide legal representation and a settlement is reached in the case, then NCDHHS and the LHD must each pay half of the settlement costs. Under certain circumstances, NCDHHS may opt to exercise its discretion to pay a larger portion of the settlement based on the unique facts of the case.[58] Recovery under the State Tort Claims Act is capped at a maximum of one million dollars.[59] For claims arising out of an REHS, REHSI, or REHSA's enforcement of *local* environmental health rules, legal representation by the AG is not provided and no portion of a settlement will be paid by NCDHHS.[60]

What happens if an LHD fails to enter into the required annual agreement with NCDHHS? In this situation, any REHS, REHSI, or REHA who works for or is contracted by that LHD would not be entitled to legal representation by the AG in lawsuits that arise from acts or omissions that occurred while the REHS, REHSI, or REHA was working for that LHD and enforcing CPH rules. The county or counties served by the LHD could defend the REHS, REHSI, or REHA, but they are not required to do so.[61] NCDHHS would also not be responsible for paying any portion of a settlement reached in a case involving an REHS, REHSI, or REHA who worked for an LHD that failed to execute the annual agreement with NCDHHS.[62]

Notes

1. The legal liability and immunity of North Carolina local governments, officials, and employees is also discussed in Kristi A. Nickodem, *Civil Liability of the Local Government and Its Officials and Employees, in* County and Municipal Government in North Carolina ch. 6 (Christopher B. McLaughlin ed., UNC School of Government, 2025 ed. 2025).
2. *See* Meyer v. Walls, 347 N.C. 97, 110 (1997) ("A suit against a defendant in his individual capacity means that the plaintiff seeks recovery from the defendant directly; a suit against a defendant in his official capacity means that the plaintiff seeks recovery from the entity of which the public servant defendant is an agent.").
3. *See* G.S. 153A-11 (granting counties authority to sue and be sued); *see also* Olavarria v. Wake Cnty. Hum. Servs., 234 N.C. App. 665 (2014) (citing Craig v. County of Chatham, 143 N.C. App. 30, 31 (2001)); Piland v. Hertford Cnty. Bd. of Comm'rs, 141 N.C. App. 293 (2000).
4. *See Meyer*, 347 N.C. at 110; G.S. 130A-36(a) (defining a district health department as a "public authority" under G.S. 159-7(b)(10)).
5. *See Meyer*, 347 N.C. at 110 (1997).
6. G.S. 132-9(c); G.S. 143-318.16B.
7. G.S. 132-9(c); G.S. 143-318.16B.
8. *Tort*, Black's Law Dictionary (12th ed. 2024).
9. *See* Nickodem, *supra* note 1, at 107.
10. A third category of torts, known as strict-liability torts, is beyond the scope of this chapter.
11. *See Negligence*, Black's Law Dictionary (12th ed. 2024).
12. *See* Block v. County of Person, 141 N.C. App. 273 (2000).
13. *See id.*; Carter v. Stanly County, 123 N.C. App. 235 (1996).
14. *See* Tabor v. County of Orange, 156 N.C. App. 88 (2003).
15. *See Tort*, Black's Law Dictionary (12th ed. 2024).
16. *See* Trey Allen, Local Government Immunity to Lawsuits in North Carolina 2 (UNC School of Government, 2018); *see also* Phillips v. Orange Cnty. Health Dep't, 237 N.C. App. 249, 256 (2014) ("[A]ny action against a local board of health, as an agency of the county, is an action against the county for the purposes of governmental immunity."); G.S. 130A-37(k) ("The purchase of liability insurance pursuant to this subsection waives both the district board of health's and the district health department's governmental immunity, to the extent of insurance coverage, for any act or omission occurring in the exercise of a governmental function.").
17. *See* Wright v. Gaston County, 205 N.C. App. 600 (2010) ("Plaintiff's complaint also alleges claims against the [defendants] in their individual capacities, for which governmental immunity is not applicable.").
18. Hart v. Brienza, 246 N.C. App. 426, 431 (2016) (quoting Smith v. State, 289 N.C. 303, 331 (1976)); *see also* Kitchin *ex rel.* Kitchin v. Halifax County, 192 N.C. App. 559, 568 (2008) (finding a local health director to be a public officer entitled to public official immunity).
19. Doe v. Wake County, 264 N.C. App. 692, 695 (2019) (quoting Hobbs *ex rel.* Winner v. N.C. Dep't of Hum. Res., 135 N.C. App. 412, 422 (1999)).
20. *See* McCullers v. Lewis, 265 N.C. App. 216, 222 (2019); Wells v. N.C. Dep't of Corr., 152 N.C. App. 307, 320 (2002). For a more comprehensive discussion of this topic, see Trey Allen, *Do Intentional Tort Claims Always Defeat Public Official Immunity?*, Loc. Gov't L. Bull. No. 139 (UNC School of Government, Sept. 2016); *see also* Trey Allen, *Public Official Immunity for Intentional Torts? The Split Continues*, Coates' Canons: NC Loc. Gov't L. (June 20, 2019), https://canons.sog.unc.edu/2019/06/public-official-immunity-for-intentional-torts-the-split-continues/.

21. *See* Wray v. City of Greensboro, 370 N.C. 41, 47 (2017). Entering into a valid contract constitutes a waiver of governmental immunity.
22. The legal liability of North Carolina local governments and local government officials and employees under Section 1983 is discussed in Nickodem, *supra* note 1.
23. *See* Monell v. Dep't of Soc. Servs., 436 U.S. 658 (1978); *see also* Hogan v. Cherokee County, 519 F. Supp. 3d 263 (W.D.N.C. 2021).
24. Mullenix v. Luna, 577 U.S. 7, 11 (2015) (citing Pearson v. Callahan, 555 U.S. 223, 231 (2009)).
25. *Id.* at 11 (quoting Reichle v. Howards, 566 U.S. 658 (2012)).
26. *Id.* at 12 (quoting Malley v. Briggs, 475 U.S. 335, 341 (1986)).
27. G.S. 14-234.
28. *Id.*
29. G.S. 143-318.17.
30. *See, e.g.*, G.S. 14, §§ 33, 34.2, 32.4.
31. G.S. 14-92.
32. G.S. 14-209.
33. G.S. 14-230(a).
34. *See, e.g.*, Phillips v. Orange Cnty. Health Dep't, 237 N.C. App. 249 (2014); Craig v. County of Chatham, 356 N.C. 40 (2002); City of Roanoke Rapids v. Peedin, 124 N.C. App. 578 (1996).
35. G.S. 130A-39(a).
36. G.S. 130A-39(c).
37. G.S. 130A-24(b).
38. G.S. 130A-24(b).
39. G.S. 130A-24(c).
40. G.S. 130A-24(d).
41. *See* Craig v. County of Chatham, 356 N.C. 40 (2002); City of Roanoke Rapids v. Peedin, 124 N.C. App. 578 (1996).
42. G.S. 153A-97.
43. G.S. 160A-167(a).
44. G.S. 130A-37(k).
45. G.S. 153A-435.
46. G.S. 130A-37(k).
47. G.S. 153A-435(a).
48. G.S. 130A-37(k).
49. The North Carolina State Tort Claims Act is codified at G.S. 143, art. 31.
50. G.S. 130A-4(b); Title 15A, Chapter 01O, Section .0100 of the North Carolina Administrative Code (hereinafter N.C.A.C.).
51. G.S. 90A, art. 4.
52. *See, e.g.*, G.S. 143-300.8.
53. 15A N.C.A.C. 01O, § .0101.
54. G.S. 90A-52(b).
55. *See* G.S. 130A-4(b), (d); G.S. 143-300.8.
56. S.L. 2024-49, sec. 4.7, § 143-300.8.
57. G.S. 143-300.4(a).
58. G.S. 143-300.8(b) to (c).
59. G.S. 143-299.2(a).
60. G.S. 143-300.8(e).
61. G.S. 153A-97.
62. G.S. 143-300.8(d).

Chapter 15
Public Health Authorities

What Is a Public Health Authority?

A public health authority (PHA) is a type of local health department (LHD) that provides public health services for one or more counties.[1] As a "public authority" under North Carolina law, a PHA is directly subject to many of the same laws that apply to other local government entities, such as laws regulating public records, open meetings, and financial management.[2]

A PHA, whether single county or multicounty, is governed by a board[3] and administered by a director (the local health director).[4] PHA boards are different in many ways from their counterparts that oversee county health departments, district health departments, and consolidated human services agencies. This is in part because state law grants PHAs a slate of unique powers and duties. For example, a PHA may purchase or finance real or personal property; sell its surplus buildings, land, or equipment; and operate health care networks.[5]

Forming, Withdrawing from, and Dissolving a Public Health Authority

The creation of a PHA that serves a single county requires a public hearing on the intent of the board of county commissioners (BOCC) to establish a PHA. The BOCC must publish notice of the public hearing at least ten days in advance of the hearing date.[6] After the hearing, the BOCC and the existing board of health (BOH) for the county must adopt a joint resolution that it is in the interest of the public health and welfare to provide public health services to the community through a PHA.[7] Once the PHA is established, the new PHA board is appointed[8] and the previous BOH is dissolved. The PHA takes on the functions, assets, and liabilities of the previous LHD and BOH.[9]

When a multicounty PHA is formed, both steps—the public hearing and the joint resolution—must be taken by every county that will participate in the PHA.[10] If a county seeks to join an existing multicounty PHA, then the joining county must also hold a properly noticed public hearing and adopt a joint resolution.[11] Once the PHA is established, the new PHA board is appointed[12] and the previous BOHs are dissolved. The PHA takes on the functions, assets, and liabilities of the previous LHDs and BOHs.[13]

Counties may also withdraw from or seek to dissolve a PHA, and the processes involved mirror those used for the withdrawal from or dissolution of a district health department. To withdraw from a multicounty PHA, the BOCC for the county seeking to withdraw must determine that the PHA is not operating in the best health interests of the county. If the BOCC for every county participating in the PHA determines that the PHA is not operating in the best health interests of its county, then the PHA may be dissolved entirely. Withdrawal from or dissolution of a PHA cannot take effect until the end of the state fiscal year.[14]

Following a withdrawal from or dissolution of a PHA, any rules adopted by the PHA board remain in effect in the county or counties that were previously part of the PHA until they are amended or repealed by a new BOH.[15] Dissolution of a PHA also requires providing prior written notice of the dissolution to the North Carolina Department of Health and Human Services.[16] State law does not require a county to give such notice before *withdrawing* from a multicounty PHA, but providing notice is a best practice. Following a withdrawal from or dissolution of a multicounty PHA, a certified public accountant or an auditor certified by the Local Government Commission distributes surplus funds to the counties according to the percentage each of the participating counties contributed during that year.[17]

Consolidation

State law prohibits a BOCC from consolidating a PHA and making it part of a consolidated human services agency.[18]

Appointment of the Board

The BOCC appoints all members of a single-county PHA board. For a multicounty PHA board, the chair of each county's BOCC appoints one of their own fellow county commissioners, or the county commissioner's designee, to the board. Those commissioners (or their designees) then appoint the remaining members of the multicounty PHA board.[19] Although not required by law, it is common practice for PHA board members to provide recommendations to the BOCC when a position on the board becomes vacant and needs to be filled.

Composition of the Board

A PHA board that serves a single county must be composed of seven to nine members. A board that serves multiple counties may include no more than eleven members.[20] In some instances, a PHA may want to apply to the federal government to become a community health center and be made eligible for additional federal funds. The federal law governing community health centers has strict requirements related to board size and composition.[21] Therefore, North Carolina law allows a PHA that is interested in becoming a community health center to have up to twenty-five board members.[22]

A PHA board must include at least the following members:

- one physician licensed to practice medicine in North Carolina,
- one dentist licensed to practice dentistry in North Carolina,
- one county commissioner (or the commissioner's designee) from each county participating in the PHA,
- one member of the general public,
- one member of the administrative staff of a hospital serving the PHA's service area, and
- any combination of two licensed or registered professionals in the fields of
    - optometry,
    - veterinary science,
    - nursing,
    - pharmacy,
    - engineering, or
    - accounting.[23]

In contrast to the laws governing county and district BOHs, the laws addressing PHA boards do not specify what action the BOCC should take if there is not a professional, such as a licensed physician, available to appoint to the PHA board. However, unlike members of county and district BOHs, members of PHA boards are not required to be residents of a county served by the PHA. As a result, the BOCC is less likely to run into the challenge of being unable to find a professional to appoint to the board.

Board Terms, Term Limits, and Removal of Members

Board members are appointed to three-year terms and the law is silent as to the maximum number of terms they may serve.[24] If a member of a PHA board vacates their position before the end of their three-year term, the person who is appointed to fill that vacancy serves for the remaining portion of the original member's three-year term. State law requires that any vacancies on a PHA board be filled within 120 days of the seat becoming vacant.[25]

A board member may be removed from office before the end of the member's term only if there is cause for removal under North Carolina law. The law states that a member may be removed for

- commission of a felony or other crime involving moral turpitude;
- violation of a state law governing conflicts of interest;
- violation of a written policy adopted by the county commissioners (or by all of the applicable boards of commissioners, if it is a multicounty board);
- habitual failure to attend meetings;
- conduct that tends to bring the office into disrepute; or
- failure to maintain the qualifications for appointment (such as maintaining a professional licensure).[26]

The law governing removal of a member requires that the member first be given written notice of the basis for the member's removal and an opportunity to respond to that written notice. A PHA board may remove a board member on its own and without requiring action by the BOCC.[27]

The Board and the Local Health Director

State law authorizes the PHA board to appoint the local health director after consultation with the BOCC(s) for the county or counties served by the PHA.[28] When a board fails to appoint a local health director within sixty days of the position becoming vacant, state law authorizes the state health director to appoint a local health director to serve in the interim until the board can make an appointment.[29]

Any person appointed to the position of local health director after January 1, 1992, must possess one of the following:[30]

- a medical doctorate;
- a master's degree in public health administration, and at least one year of employment experience in health programs or health services;
- a master's degree in a public health discipline other than public health administration, and at least three years of employment experience in health programs or health services;
- a master's degree in public administration, and at least two years of experience in health programs or health services;
- a master's degree in a field related to public health, and at least three years of experience in health programs or health services; or
- a bachelor's degree in public health administration or public administration and at least three years of experience in health programs or health services.

Advance review and approval by the state health director is required if the board wishes to appoint a candidate whose eligibility is predicated on a master's degree in a field related to public health and at least three years of experience in health programs or services. In this situation, the board must send the state health director a copy of the candidate's application and any other pertinent materials for review. If the state health director determines that the candidate's master's degree is not in a field related to public health, then the state health director must notify the board in writing within fifteen days of receiving the candidate's application and materials. Otherwise, the candidate is considered to have satisfied the educational requirements, and the board may proceed with appointing the candidate to the position.[31]

The Board and Fees

A PHA board's role in setting fees and the limits on the board's authority to set fees are generally the same as those for a county, district, or consolidated human services board (see Chapter 9). There is one key difference: PHA boards are not required to obtain BOCC approval of the fee schedules that they create.[32]

Ethics

A PHA board's ethical obligations are generally the same as those of a county, district, or consolidated human services board (see Chapter 11). One key difference is that PHA boards have the authority to independently enter into contracts,[33] which has implications for certain state laws governing conflicts of interest and opportunities for board members to benefit, directly or indirectly, from contracts.

Open Meetings and Public Records

A PHA board is generally subject to the same laws pertaining to open meetings (see Chapter 12) and public records (see Chapter 13) as a county, district, or consolidated human services board. However, while the records of county health department, district health department, and consolidated human services agency employees are governed by G.S. 153A-98, the confidentiality of PHA personnel information is governed by separate statutes, found in G.S. Chapter 130A.[34]

Liability and Immunity

A PHA's employees and its board may enjoy governmental immunity and public official immunity as described in Chapter 14. Additionally, state law authorizes PHAs to purchase insurance policies for their employees, board members, and agents and describes limits on the scope of those policies.[35]

Accreditation, Rulemaking, and Adjudications

In other respects, the information in this book pertaining to other types of BOHs is equally applicable to PHA boards, including accreditation (see Chapter 7), rulemaking (Chapter 8), and adjudications (Chapter 10).

Notes

1. Chapter 130A, Section 2(5) of the North Carolina General Statutes (hereinafter G.S.).
2. G.S. 130A-45.02(g) (citing G.S. 159-7(b)(10) (defining *public authority*)). For more information about public authorities, see Kara Millonzi, *Special Purpose Local Governments and Public Authorities*, Coates' Canons: NC Loc. Gov't L. (Feb. 10, 2015), https://canons.sog.unc.edu/2015/02/special-purpose-local-governments-and-public-authorities/.
3. G.S. 130A-45.1.
4. G.S. 130A, §§ 45.4, 45.5.
5. G.S. 130A-45.3.
6. G.S. 130A-45.02(h).
7. G.S. 130A-45.02(a).
8. G.S. 130A-45.02(c).
9. G.S. 130A-45.02(f).
10. G.S. 130A-45.02(b).
11. G.S. 130A-45.02(d).
12. G.S. 130A-45.02(c).
13. G.S. 130A-45.02(f).
14. G.S. 130A-45.2(a).
15. G.S. 130A-45.2(d).
16. G.S. 130A-45.2(b).
17. G.S. 130A-45.2(c).
18. G.S. 153A-76(5).
19. G.S. 130A-45.1(b).
20. G.S. 130A-45.1(a).
21. 42 C.F.R. §§ 51c.304, 56.304.
22. G.S. 130A-45.1(a).
23. G.S. 130A-45.1(c).
24. G.S. 130A-45.1(d).
25. G.S. 130A-45.1(g).
26. G.S. 130A-45.1(j).
27. *Id.*
28. G.S. 130A-45.4(a).
29. G.S. 130A-45.4(e).
30. G.S. 130A-45.4(b). In 2024, S.L. 2024-34, Section 3.(a) amended the experience and education requirements for a local health director in a county or district health department or consolidated human services agency. The same changes were not made to the statute (G.S. 130A-45.4) that sets the experience and education requirements for a local health director serving in a PHA.
31. G.S. 130A-45.4(c).
32. G.S. 130A-45.3(a)(5).
33. G.S. 130A-45.3(a)(12).
34. *See, e.g.*, G.S. 130A, §§ 45.9, 45.10, 45.12.
35. G.S. 130A-45.3(g) to (h).

Chapter 16
Hospital Authorities

What Is a Hospital Authority?

A hospital authority is a type of special-purpose local government (sometimes referred to as a *public authority*).[1] The purpose of a hospital authority is to "provide an alternate method for counties and cities to provide hospital, medical, and health care."[2] A hospital authority may be established when a city council (which is defined to include a town council[3]) or a board of county commissioners (BOCC) adopts a resolution finding that creating the hospital authority is "in the interest of the public health and welfare."[4]

Hospital Authorities and Local Public Health

The county health department, the district health department, the public health authority, and the public health component of a consolidated human services agency exist solely to provide public health services. By contrast, a county hospital authority may—but does not have to—take on the powers, duties, and responsibilities of a local health department (LHD), but only if the hospital authority meets certain requirements set forth in an uncodified 1997 state law.[5]

Specifically, the county hospital authority board must be composed of no more than seven members and must have been established on or before July 1, 1997, under the provisions of Chapter 131E, Article 2, Part 2 of the North Carolina General Statutes (hereinafter G.S.). The law also requires that the decision to provide public health services for the county through the hospital authority be memorialized in a resolution adopted by the BOCC and approved by the state health director.[6]

Few North Carolina counties have a hospital authority that is eligible to operate as the county's LHD. However, any county may establish a public health authority, which has several traits in common with a hospital authority.[7] Like a public health authority, a hospital authority is a "public authority" and is therefore subject to many of the same laws that apply to local government entities, such as public records laws, open meetings laws, and certain financial management laws.[8]

In other ways, a hospital authority that operates as an LHD is different from a public health authority and other types of LHD. For example, a hospital authority's jurisdiction may extend ten miles beyond the county's border;[9] a hospital authority can borrow money[10] and exercise the governmental power of eminent domain;[11] and a hospital authority has numerous responsibilities and powers related to the operation and staffing of a hospital.[12]

Appointment of Board Members

The governing body for a hospital authority is a hospital authority board, which is composed of members who are referred to as *commissioners*. A hospital authority board cannot have less than six or more than thirty commissioners.[13] If a hospital authority was established by a BOCC in a county with a population greater than 75,000, then the commissioners for the hospital authority board are appointed by the BOCC chair.[14] If a hospital authority was established by a BOCC in a county with a population less than 75,000, then the commissioners for the hospital authority board are appointed by the BOCC as a group (not solely by the BOCC chair).[15]

When a county hospital authority board is first established, the chair of the board is selected by the BOCC chair (regardless of the size of the county's population). All subsequent chairs are chosen by their fellow commissioners on the hospital authority board.[16]

Terms, Vacancies, and Removal of Members

When a hospital authority is first established, the commissioners on the hospital authority board must be appointed to terms of different lengths to ensure staggered terms. A third of the commissioners must be appointed to one-year terms, one-third to two-year terms, and the remaining third to three-year terms. All subsequent appointments are for three-year terms.

If a seat on the hospital authority board becomes vacant, it must be filled for the remaining (unexpired) portion of the term.[17] If a hospital authority was created by a BOCC of a county with a population greater than 75,000, the BOCC chair must fill any hospital authority board vacancies by selecting from a slate of nominees put forth by the hospital authority board's current commissioners.[18] If a hospital authority was created by the BOCC of a county with a population less than 75,000, then the BOCC must consider any nominees suggested by the current commissioners but can ultimately choose any qualified person to fill a board vacancy.[19]

The person or entity that appoints the commissioners of a county hospital authority board (BOCC chair or BOCC, as applicable) is the party authorized by law to remove commissioners from the board. A commissioner may be removed for "inefficiency, neglect of duty, or misconduct in office."[20] "Misconduct in office" can include violations of certain provisions of the hospital authority conflict-of-interest law at G.S. 131E-22.[21] Removal of a commissioner from the hospital authority board must be carried out in compliance with the process set forth at G.S. 131E-22.

Notes

1. Kara Millonzi, *Special Purpose Local Governments and Public Authorities*, Coates' Canons: NC Loc. Gov't L. (Feb. 10, 2015), https://canons.sog.unc.edu/2015/02/special-purpose-local-governments-and-public-authorities/.
2. Chapter 131E, Section 15(b) of the North Carolina General Statutes (hereinafter G.S.).
3. *See* G.S. 131E-16(5) (*city council* means the "body charged with governing the city or town").
4. G.S. 131E-17(a).
5. S.L. 1997-502, § 12.
6. *Id.*
7. For more information about public health authorities, see G.S. 130A, §§ 45–45.13 and Chapter 15 of this book.
8. *See generally*, Millonzi, *supra* note 1 (discussing public authorities).
9. G.S. 131E-20.
10. G.S. 131E-23(a)(8).
11. G.S. 131E-24.
12. G.S. 131E-23.
13. G.S. 131E-18(a).
14. G.S. 131E, §§ 17(b), 18(a).
15. G.S. 131E, §§ 17(b), 18(g)(1).
16. G.S. 131E-18(c).
17. G.S. 131E-18(b).
18. G.S. 131E-18(d).
19. G.S. 131E-18(g)(2). The laws governing hospital authorities do not define what it means to be "qualified" to serve as a commissioner on a hospital authority board.
20. G.S. 131E-22(a).
21. G.S. 131E-21(c).

Appendix A
Selected Resources for Board Members

For the most up-to-date resources that may be relevant to local boards of health, please visit the **North Carolina Human Services Hub** at humanservices.sog.unc.edu. Selected additional resources that may be useful to local boards of health are listed by topic below. All web addresses are current as of May 2025.

Consolidated Human Services Agencies

Kristi A. Nickodem, *Personnel Decisions for North Carolina's Consolidated Human Services Agencies*, Social Services Bulletin 49 (UNC School of Government, 2021), https://www.sog.unc.edu/publications/bulletins/personnel-decisions-north-carolinas-consolidated-human-services-agencies.

Ethics

A. Fleming Bell, II, *Ethics, Conflicts, and Offices: A Guide for Local Officials*, 2nd ed. (UNC School of Government, 2011).

Kristina M. Wilson and Crista Cuccaro, "Ethics and Conflicts of Interest," in *County and Municipal Government in North Carolina*, 2025 ed., edited by Christopher B. McLaughlin (UNC School of Government, 2025).

Hiring and Evaluating the Director

Diane M. Juffras, *Recruitment and Selection Law for Local Government Employers* (UNC School of Government, 2013).

"Prohibited Employment Policies/Practices," U.S. Equal Employment Opportunity Commission, https://www.eeoc.gov/prohibited-employment-policiespractices, archived April 23, 2025 at https://perma.cc/3FJB-AJ8W.

Vaughn Mamlin Upshaw, *How Are We Doing? Evaluating Manager and Board Performance* (UNC School of Government, 2014).

Vaughn Mamlin Upshaw, John A. Rible IV, and Carl W. Stenberg, *Getting the Right Fit: The Governing Board's Role in Hiring a Manager* (UNC School of Government, 2011).

Note: *How Are We Doing?* and *Getting the Right Fit* discuss hiring and evaluating a county manager, but some of the concepts may be useful for recruiting and evaluating the local health director.

Liability

Trey Allen, *Local Government Immunity to Lawsuits in North Carolina* (UNC School of Government, 2018).

Kristi A. Nickodem, "Civil Liability of the Local Government and Its Officials and Employees," in *County and Municipal Government in North Carolina*, 2025 ed., edited by Christopher B. McLaughlin (UNC School of Government, 2025).

Open Meetings

Trey Allen, *"Full and Accurate" Minutes: A Primer*, Local Government Law Bulletin 140 (UNC School of Government, January 2019), https://www.sog.unc.edu/publications/bulletins/full-and-accurate-minutes-primer.

Frayda S. Bluestein and David M. Lawrence, *Open Meetings and Local Governments in North Carolina: Some Questions and Answers*, 8th ed. (UNC School of Government, 2017).

Kristina M. Wilson, "Open Meetings and Other Legal Requirements for Local Government Boards," in *County and Municipal Government in North Carolina*, 2025 ed., edited by Christopher B. McLaughlin (UNC School of Government, 2025.

Public Records

Kristina M. Wilson, "Public Records," in *County and Municipal Government in North Carolina*, 2025 ed., edited by Christopher B. McLaughlin (UNC School of Government, 2025).

David M. Lawrence, *Public Records Law for North Carolina Local Governments*, 2nd ed. (UNC School of Government, 2009).

Records Retention

"Local Government Agencies," State Archives of North Carolina, North Carolina Department of Natural and Cultural Resources, https://archives.ncdcr.gov/government/local.

Rules of Procedure

Trey Allen and A. Fleming Bell, II, *Suggested Procedural Rules for Local Appointed Boards* (UNC School of Government, 2020).

Public Health

Association of North Carolina Boards of Health, https://www.ancbh.org/.

Jill D. Moore, *Local Boards of Health in North Carolina: Overview of Membership Requirements and Legal Authorities* (UNC School of Government, May 2018), https://www.sog.unc.edu/resources/microsites/north-carolina-public-health-law/boards-health-north-carolina.

Jill D. Moore, *North Carolina Communicable Disease Law* (UNC School of Government, 2017).

Jill D. Moore and Kirsten E. Leloudis, "Public Health," in *County and Municipal Government in North Carolina*, 2025 ed., edited by Christopher B. McLaughlin (UNC School of Government, 2025).

Coates' Canons Selected Posts

Coates' Canons (canons.sog.unc.edu) is a UNC School of Government blog featuring blog posts from School of Government faculty regarding legal issues affecting local governments and other public agencies in North Carolina. The list below is a small sampling of hundreds of posts that may be useful to local health directors and board members. Individuals can subscribe to the blog, search posts by keyword, and browse posts by topic categories.

Posts by Frayda S. Bluestein

"How to Approve Minutes and General Accounts of Closed Sessions," June 5, 2018, https://canons.sog.unc.edu/2018/06/how-to-approve-minutes-and-general-accounts-of-closed-sessions/.

"Retention Schedules for Local Governments: Five Things You Should Know," May 16, 2019, https://canons.sog.unc.edu/2019/05/retention-schedules-for-local-governments-five-things-you-should-know/.

"Setting Salaries and Closed Sessions," December 17, 2015, https://canons.sog.unc.edu/2015/12/setting-salaries-and-closed-sessions/.

"Quick Reference Guide for Closed Sessions," March 13, 2014, https://canons.sog.unc.edu/2014/03/quick-reference-guide-for-closed-session-meetings/.

Posts by Kirsten E. Leloudis

"S.L. 2024-34: Impacts for Local Health Directors," September 4, 2024, https://canons.sog.unc.edu/2024/09/s-l-2024-34-local-health-directors/.

"Do Local Health Directors Need to Take an Oath of Office?" February 9, 2024, https://canons.sog.unc.edu/2024/02/health-director-oath/.

Posts by Kristina M. Wilson

"The Court of Appeals Addresses Emergency Meetings and Remote Quorum," August 13, 2024, https://canons.sog.unc.edu/2024/08/the-court-of-appeals-addresses-emergency-meetings-and-remote-quorum/.

"Closed Session Deep Dive: Privileged or Confidential Information," August 1, 2024, https://canons.sog.unc.edu/2024/08/closed-session-deep-dive-privileged-or-confidential-information/.
"Closed Session Deep Dive: Attorney-Client Privilege," May 7, 2024, https://canons.sog.unc.edu/2024/05/closed-session-deep-dive-attorney-client-privilege/.
"Closed Session Deep Dive: Personnel Matters," (April 1, 2024), https://canons.sog.unc.edu/2024/04/closed-session-deep-dive-personnel-matters/.